Faux Finishing
for the first time™

Faux Finishing
for the first time™

Rhonda Rainey

Sterling Publishing Co., Inc.
New York
A Sterling / Chapelle Book

Chapelle:

Jo Packham, Owner

Cathy Sexton, Editor

Staff: Ann Bear, Areta Bingham, Kass Burchett, Marilyn Goff, Holly Hollingsworth, Will Jones, Susan Jorgensen, Barbara Milburn, Linda Orton, Karmen Quinney, Leslie Ridenour, Cindy Stoeckl, Gina Swapp, Sara Toliver

Photography: Kevin Dilley for Hazen Imaging, Inc.
Gallery Photography: Various professional photographers unknown by name, unless indicated.
Photo on Cover: Charger was stippled with dark crimson and metallic gold acrylic paints.

If rubber cement is not available in your area, consult any craft store to find a comparable product.

If you have any questions or comments or would like information on specialty products featured in this book, please contact Chapelle, Ltd., Inc., P.O. Box 9252, Ogden, UT 84409 • (801) 621-2777 • (801) 621-2788 Fax • e-mail: chapelle@chapelleltd.com • website: www.chapelleltd.com

Library of Congress Cataloging-in-Publication Data
    Rainey, Rhonda.
       Faux finishing for the first time / Rhonda Rainey.
          p.   cm.
       "A Sterling/Chapelle book."
       Includes index.
       ISBN 0-8069-4483-8 Hardcover
       ISBN 1-4027-0885-8 Paperback
       1. Painting.   2. Decoration and ornament.   3. Finishes and finishing.   I. Title.

TT385.R35 2000   00-033896
745.7'23--dc21   CIP

10 9 8 7 6 5 4 3 2 1

First paperback edition published in 2003 by
Sterling Publishing Co., Inc.
387 Park Avenue South, New York, NY 10016
© 2000 by Rhonda Rainey
Distributed in Canada by Sterling Publishing
c/o Canadian Manda Group, One Atlantic Avenue, Suite 105
Toronto, Ontario, Canada M6K 3E7
Distributed in Great Britain by Chrysalis Books
64 Brewery Road, London N7 9NT, England
Distributed in Australia by Capricorn Link (Australia) Pty Ltd.
P.O. Box 704, Windsor, NSW 2756, Australia
Printed in China
All Rights Reserved

Sterling ISBN 0-8069-4483-8 Hardcover
            1-4027-0885-5 Paperback

About the author

Rhonda Rainey is an artist of many interests and talents. She is an award-winning watercolorist, designer, and published author.

Those associated with Rhonda find her to be thoughtful and innovative when it comes to pushing the boundaries of established crafting techniques. She approaches each new project with a fresh and spirited perspective.

An art educator for more than 20 years, Rhonda is currently working as a freelance artist and designer. Occasionally she returns to the classroom as a substitute teacher "to keep one foot" in the real world.

The mother of three grown children, and a fun-loving grandmother, she resides in Pocatello, Idaho.

This book is dedicated to those I love. You know who you are.

Acknowledgments

Special thanks to my family and friends for their love, support, and encouragement.

Heartfelt thanks to Jo Packham and the staff at Chapelle for their friendship and for helping me find my wings.

My appreciation to editor, Cathy Sexton, who "shared the vision." Her suggestions and skills made this project a positive learning experience.

A huge thank-you to the artists who contributed their beautiful work and shared their ideas in the gallery.

Table of Contents

Faux finishing for the first time

Introduction

Since the beginning of time, human beings have been decorating their dwellings. History shows us that the first artists painted images of the outside world, hunting scenes, and daily life on the walls of their caves. These paintings may have had ritual or religious meanings, or they may have been created simply to enhance the surroundings of those who lived there. Whatever their purpose, the decorative arts, in one form or another, have been a part of all cultures from earliest times.

Faux (pronounced foe) painting, found as early as the times of the ancient Romans, has enjoyed continued popularity in all parts of the world. In the 1800s, faux painting was no longer reserved for the homes of nobility and aristocracy. Schools were founded, craftsmen trained, and art materials became readily available.

The 20th century has brought great advancements in the manufacturing of paints, especially those made from synthetic binders. These are commonly called latex or emulsion paints. They are durable, safe, easy to use, and their color range is limited only by the imagination. As a craft, faux finishing is enjoying more popularity than ever because of these materials, the availability of information, and leisure time to pursue those things which interest us.

How to use this book

The purpose of this book is to inspire and encourage the person who wants to try faux finishing, but fears that they have no artistic ability. Expertise is not required, but a desire to try something new and unfamiliar is. Great results can be achieved if you are willing to experiment a little and to use your imagination. A little practice and confidence will go a long way toward producing pleasing and exciting results.

The techniques are shown step-by-step on practice boards and have been organized in the order of difficulty. Those techniques which are most difficult will involve more steps and may include several painting techniques. Choose projects for your level of ability and then expand! I would suggest making practice boards of your own. Paint two coats of white latex or acrylic craft paint on a piece of poster board. Try the techniques on the board before you begin the actual project. If it doesn't work as you had anticipated, try again. Learn to enjoy the process as well as the final result—you might even invent a new technique.

As you look through this book, you will find that I have used a number of different paint effects on all types of surfaces—wood, glass and ceramic, metal, and wax. The projects I have chosen use inexpensive items that have character; many of them can be found in second-hand and thrift stores. I believe there is less "fear of failure" when you start with something that is not expensive. The transformation is pure excitement!

The painting mediums used in this book are all water-based (acrylic, latex, emulsion). They were chosen because they are easy to use and they clean up with water. They also dry quickly, so more than one coat can be applied in a relatively short period of time. In addition, water-based paints are available in several finishes, including flat, satin (or eggshell), semigloss, and gloss. Most of the projects were also sealed with a water-based varnish to help protect them, in addition to enhance their appearance. However, a solvent-based (oil, polyurethane) varnish should be used when vinegar painting.

Section 1: This section will familiarize you with the faux-finishing basics, from essential tools and supplies to instructions on the preparation of surfaces to be faux finished. Additionally, each technique gives a list of specific items you will need for that project.

Section 2: This section teaches some basic faux-finishing techniques. It is recommended that you practice each method on a practice board before applying the finish to your project.

Section 3: This section teaches techniques beyond the basics; ones that would be considered more advanced. In some of these projects, more than one technique has been combined.

Section 4: The gallery section presented is pure inspiration! It is important to understand that the purpose of this publication is to teach basic faux finishes to those attempting them for the first time. It takes a great deal of practice before one would be able to achieve some of the advanced finishes shown. We included them strictly for your enjoyment. Many thanks to the artists and designers who contributed photographs of their work.

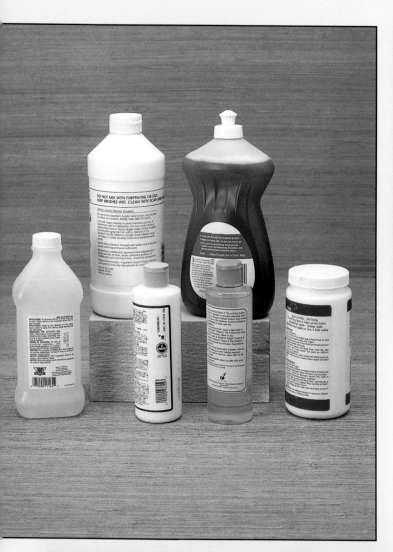

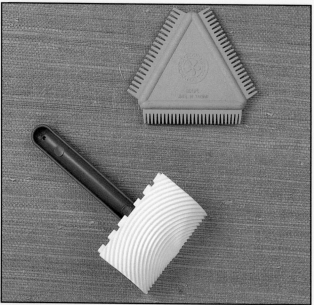

Section 1:
faux-finish basics

What tools and supplies do I need to get started?

Having the right tools and supplies for the job can mean the difference between success and an ongoing struggle with your project. Everything that is needed can be purchased at a hardware, paint, or craft store.

The following list of tools and supplies is necessary for creating faux-finished projects. In addition, each technique gives a list of other items needed for that specific project.

1 Newspaper
Newspaper is used to cover work surfaces to protect them.

2 Chemical Stripping Agent
A chemical stripping agent is a gel-type liquid that is brushed on. It is used to chemically loosen stain, paint, and varnish.

3 Paint Scraper
A paint scraper is used to remove loose patches of paint that are peeling and/or chipping. It is also used to remove paint that has been treated with a chemical stripping agent.

4 Sandpaper
Sandpaper is used to sand surfaces, most often to smooth rough areas. When sanding wood, make certain to sand with the grain of the wood. Sandpaper is available in several grades or grits. The smaller the number the coarser the grit; the larger the number the finer the grit.

5 Tack cloth
A tack cloth is used to remove excess dust from sanded surfaces.

6 Plastic scouring pad
A plastic scouring pad is used to buff very fine surfaces.

7 Putty
Putty is a latex wood filler used to fill cracks and/or holes on wooden surfaces.

8 Putty Knife
A putty knife is used to apply putty into cracks and/or holes when making repairs on wooden surfaces.

9 Paint Thinner
Paint thinner is used to wipe down the sanded wooden surfaces, prior to sealing with primer.

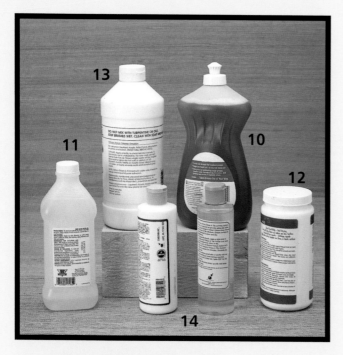

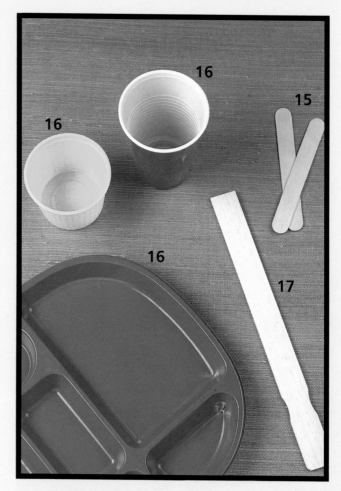

10 Dishwashing Detergent
Dishwashing detergent in a tub of hot water is used to clean the outer surfaces of glass, ceramic, and metal objects.

11 Rubbing Alcohol
Rubbing alcohol is used as a cleaning agent for removing oils and surface soils. It is also used to remove acrylic craft paint from paintbrushes and other tools. Rubbing alcohol is also known as methylated spirits.

12 Découpage Medium
In this application, découpage medium mixed with water is used as a primer for glass, ceramic, and metal objects. It works nicely for other surfaces as well and does not chip and/or scratch as easily as some primers do. In addition, it is oftentimes used as a sealer.

13 Gesso
Gesso is an all-around, first-step primer and sealer that is used to prepare surfaces to be painted.

14 Primer
Primer is a sealing coat that is brushed on. It is used primarily to seal wooden surfaces.

15 Craft Sticks
A craft stick is used to stir two or more painting mediums that have been combined in a disposable cup or bowl.

16 Disposable Cup, Bowl, and Plate
A disposable cup is used for holding two or more painting mediums so they can be thoroughly mixed. A disposable bowl is used in a similar manner, but is more convenient when a texturing medium, such as sand, is added to the painting mediums. A disposable plate is used as a palette to hold paint. Its broad surface can be accessed easily with a paintbrush or a sponge.

17 Stirring Stick
A stirring stick is used to stir and mix paint in the can.

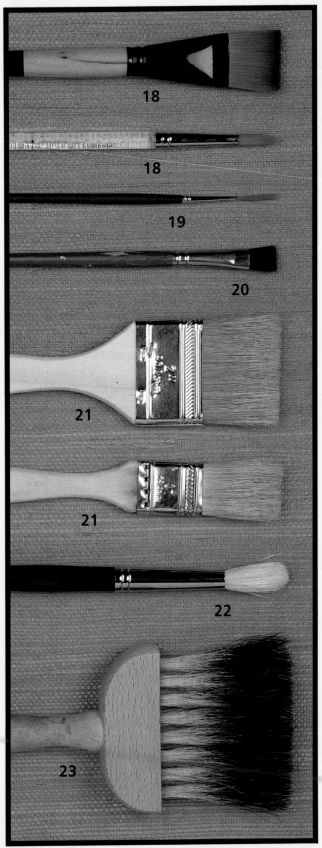

18 Soft-bristle Paintbrushes

Soft-bristle watercolor-type paintbrushes are used as the paintbrush of choice for the majority of these projects. Because of the softness of the bristle, in comparison to the bristles of oil-painting-type paintbrushes, they can be used for several painting applications and techniques. They are most generally used for applying base coats of paint to projects. They come in a variety of sizes in both flat and round shapes. Use synthetic soft-bristle paintbrushes; camel-hair or squirrel-hair paintbrushes should not be used because they shed their bristles.

19 Liner Paintbrushes

Liner paintbrushes are used for detail painting on projects. A liner paintbrush is also used for gently applying rubbing alcohol to the painted surface when creating a tortoiseshell pattern on a project.

20 Stiff-bristle Paintbrushes

Flat stiff-bristle paintbrushes are used primarily for spattering projects.

21 China-bristle Paintbrushes

China-bristle paintbrushes are used to apply coats of varnish to projects. These paintbrushes can be found in hardware stores and are inexpensive. China-bristle paintbrushes hold up well and have the right amount of spring to cover surfaces nicely. They would be classified as "not soft, not stiff"—an in-between bristle. The bristles are tapered on the tip so brushmarks are not left after each brushstroke. They come in a variety of sizes in both flat and round shapes.

22 Scumbling Paintbrushes

Scumbling paintbrushes are used primarily for stippling projects.

23 Softening Paintbrushes

Softening paintbrushes are used primarily to soften and blend colors. Their bristles are fine-textured.

24 Satin-finish Latex Paint

Satin-finish latex paint is used as the base coat for some projects after they have been primed.

25 Acrylic Craft Paints

Acrylic craft paints are used as the paint of choice for the majority of these projects, mostly because they are water-based. These paints render an even, flat finish. A vast array of colors is available.

26 Mixing Glaze

Mixing glaze is used with many faux-finishing techniques because it extends the drying time of the paint to which it has been added. In addition, the mixing glaze gives the paint color a more translucent look. Because the glaze causes acrylic craft paint to dry to a softer finish, it is important to seal with a water-based varnish. Mixing glaze will not yellow with age and it has no strong fumes.

27 Crackle Medium

Crackle medium is used to give the project a weathered and aged appearance. It is available in one- and two-part products. Some produce fine, delicate cracks while others produce a much heavier crack.

28 Tinting Medium

Tinting medium is used to give the project a pearlescent glaze look. Generally it is used as a top coat so its specialized light-refracting properties can be seen at their best. Tinting mediums are available in a number of colors and they add an elegant and sophisticated look to many surfaces.

29 Water-based Varnish

Water-based varnish is used as the varnish of choice for the majority of these projects because it is formulated to work with latex/acrylic paints. Water-based varnish also has less toxicity than solvent-based varnish and it can be cleaned up with warm, soapy water. It is quick-drying, and though it appears "milky" in the container, it dries to a clear, hard finish. Acrylic craft paint, tinting medium, and powder pigment can be used to tint water-based varnish. It is heat- and water-resistant and is available in matte, satin, or gloss finishes. Water-based varnish will not yellow with age and because most now have UV protection, the colors of paint underneath remain true and will not fade in sunlight. Water-based varnish is also available in a spray.

30 Solvent-based Varnish
Solvent-based varnish is used to seal vinegar-painted projects because water-based varnish will dissolve the vinegar paint.

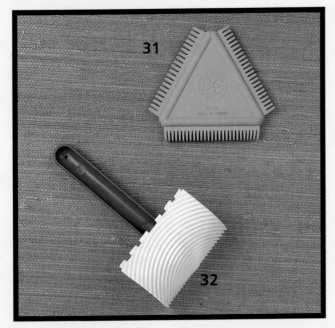

31 Rubber Combing Tool
A rubber combing tool is used to produce a striped pattern with very slight texture on flat, smooth surfaces. Metal combing tools are also available, but are more difficult to use because they are so rigid.

32 Graining Tool
A graining tool is used to create a wood-grain pattern with a very slight texture on flat, smooth surfaces. It is available with or without a handle.

33 Natural Sea Sponge
A natural sea sponge is used for applying paint to surfaces. A natural sea sponge is softer than a synthetic sponge and it makes a wonderful random pattern.

34 Synthetic Sponge
A synthetic sponge can also be used to apply paint. This sponge is firmer than a natural sea sponge and makes a more precise, repeat pattern.

35 Wedge-shaped Cosmetic Sponge
A wedge-shaped cosmetic sponge is used primarily for stenciling projects. Because it is a compact sponge, it distributes the paint more uniformly.

How do I prepare surfaces for faux finishing?

In order to achieve successful end results with faux-finish techniques, it is important to have a good start. That start does not have to be perfect, however it does require some time and work. The following list of surfaces and their preparation will help you begin with confidence.

Wood

Wood furniture and accessories which are new and unfinished, and are going to be entirely covered with paint, generally require only a single coat of primer.

If you wish to see some of the wood grain, as in a distressed finish, seal the piece of furniture or accessory with diluted varnish. Then lightly sand with fine-grit sandpaper and wipe with a tack cloth.

Old wood which has been previously stained, painted, or varnished is best stripped with a chemical stripping agent. Do not use a heat gun on old wood because many older paints contained lead and the fumes can be extremely toxic. Use plenty of paper towels and newspaper to scrape the paint residue onto and dispose of properly.

After most of the paint has been removed, use a plastic scouring pad, working with the grain of the wood, to continue removing the old finish. A stiff toothbrush works well for areas which are difficult to get into. It may be necessary to repeat the stripper application and removal several times to achieve a clean surface.

When the surface is dry, smooth with a medium-grit sandpaper, then wipe down with paint thinner. Seal with primer, then base-coat.

For a more professional look use a putty knife to fill the holes and/or cracks in the wood with putty. Wipe away excess and let dry. If the area "sinks," reapply putty and let dry. Sand until smooth, then wipe down with paint thinner. Seal with a primer, then base-coat.

If the stripping process seems like too much work and the previous paint application is in good shape, it may be possible to sand lightly and wipe with a tack cloth.

Glass and Ceramic

Glass and ceramic surfaces require a thorough cleaning with dishwashing detergent in a tub of hot water. Let dry, then wipe outer surface of project with a paper towel soaked with rubbing alcohol. When necessary, make certain to clean all crevices and detailed areas.

Using a craft stick and a disposable cup, mix two parts découpage medium with one part water. Mix well.

Using a 1" China-bristle paintbrush, apply two coats of diluted découpage medium as a primer. Let dry, then base-coat.

Metal

New metal surfaces require a thorough cleaning with dishwashing detergent in a tub of hot water. Let dry thoroughly, then wipe outer surface of project with a paper towel soaked with rubbing alcohol. When necessary, make certain to clean all crevices and detailed areas.

Let dry, then sand with medium-grit sandpaper. Wipe again with a paper towel soaked with rubbing alcohol.

Using a craft stick and a disposable cup, mix two parts découpage medium with one part water. Mix well.

Using a 1" China-bristle paintbrush, apply a coat of diluted découpage medium as a primer. Let dry, then base-coat.

Old metal may be sanded with medium-grit sandpaper, wiped down with a paper towel soaked with rubbing alcohol, then primed with diluted découpage medium.

Wax

A wax surface will generally repel paint. However, to make certain that even thinned acrylic craft paint will adhere, prepare candles as follows. Using a 3/4" soft-bristle paintbrush, apply two coats of undiluted découpage medium to outer surface of project.

Section 2: *basic techniques*

How do I spatter paint over the surfaces of an object?

A small, stiff-bristle paintbrush allows a controlled application of paint. When the brush is held close to the surface, the spatter has a more concentrated appearance. Layering colors adds depth and interest. What could be easier?

What You Need To Get Started:

Acrylic craft paints:
   beige; black; gold;
   dark green; maroon
Craft sticks
Disposable cup
Disposable plate
Newspaper
Paintbrushes:
   1/4" flat stiff-bristle;
   3/4" flat soft-bristle
Primer
Sandpaper,
   fine-grit
Tack cloth
Water-based
   spray varnish,
   matte finish
Wooden bowl,
   unfinished

Spattered Bowl

Here's How:

1. Paint the Bowl

1. Prepare bowl, following How do I prepare surfaces for faux finishing? Wood instructions on page 17.

2. Using a ³/₄" soft-bristle paintbrush, apply a base coat of beige paint to inside of bowl. Let dry. Apply a second coat and let dry.

3. Using a craft stick and a disposable cup, mix equal parts of black and dark green paints. Mix well.

4. Apply a base coat of black/dark green paint mixture to outside of bowl. Let dry. Apply a second coat and let dry.

1. 2

2. Spatter the Bowl

1. Using newspaper, cover work surface to protect it.

2. Slightly dilute black/dark green paint mixture with water.

3. Load a ¹/₄" stiff-bristle paintbrush with diluted black/dark green paint mixture.

4. Hold paintbrush in the hand you do not use to write. Hold it about 6" away with bristles pointed toward bowl. Pull the index finger of your writing hand across the bristles of the wet paintbrush, causing paint to spatter onto inside of bowl. Let dry.

Note: The size of spatters depends on the amount of water used to dilute the paint—using more water results in larger spatters; less water results in smaller spatters.

2. 4

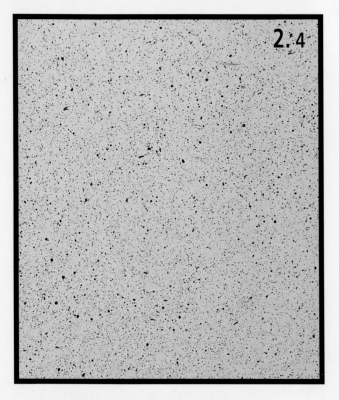

2.4

5. Repeat with diluted maroon paint. Let dry.

6. Repeat with diluted gold paint. Let dry.

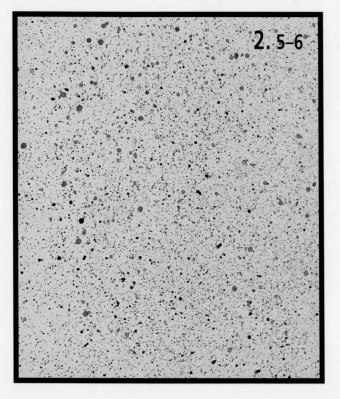

2.5–6

7. Turn bowl upside down on newspaper.

8. Slightly dilute beige paint with water.

9. Spatter outside of bowl. Let dry.

10. Repeat with diluted maroon paint. Let dry.

11. Repeat with diluted gold paint. Let dry.

12. When bowl is thoroughly dry, turn bowl right side up.

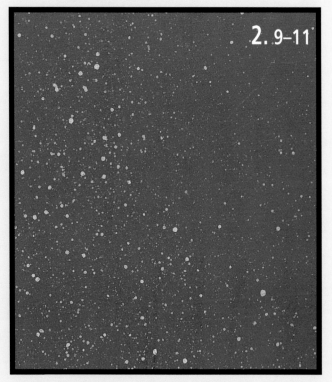

2.9–11

3. Seal the Bowl

1. Using water-based spray varnish, apply a light, even coat to inner and outer surfaces of bowl to seal. Let dry.

2. Using sandpaper, lightly buff inner and outer surfaces of bowl.

3. Using a tack cloth, wipe bowl to remove excess dust.

4. Apply a second coat of spray varnish. Let dry.

   Note: This is a decorative finish only. Food should not be served from this bowl.

23

2
technique

**What You Need
To Get Started:**

Cardboard
Copper wire,
   18-gauge*
Craft stick
Découpage medium,
   matte finish
Dishwashing detergent
Disposable cup
Glass vase
Newspaper
Paintbrush,
   1" flat China-bristle
Paper towels
Rubbing alcohol
Textured spray paint,
   rust suede
Twigs*
Wire cutters*

*Optional

How do I achieve the look of suede using textured spray paint?

Adding a unique texture to home accessories is as easy as pushing a button. The beauty and depth of suede can now be achieved with a can of spray paint. The twig and wire collar add an unexpected twist.

Suede-look Vase

Here's How:

1. Texture the Vase

   1. Prepare vase, following How do I prepare surfaces for faux finishing? Glass and Ceramic instructions on page 17.

   2. Using newspaper, cover work surface to protect it from overspray.

   3. Using a piece of cardboard, test the textured spray paint.

      Note: Make certain to work in a well-ventilated area.

   4. Spray vase with textured spray paint, following manufacturer's instructions. Let dry.

1. 4

2. Make the Twig Collar (Optional)

   1. Using wire cutters, cut several twigs approximately 3" in length.

   2. Cut two lengths of copper wire four times the circumference of the vase.

   3. Using one length of copper wire, and beginning about 1" from the top of the first twig, wrap wire around twig twice, leaving a short tail. Repeat, adding one twig at a time until collar fits around vase. See Diagram A below.

   4. Repeat, using the second length of copper wire, this time beginning about 1" from the bottom of the first twig.

   5. Wrap collar around vase, then twist wire tails together to secure in place.

   6. Trim off excess wire and tuck twisted tails behind twigs.

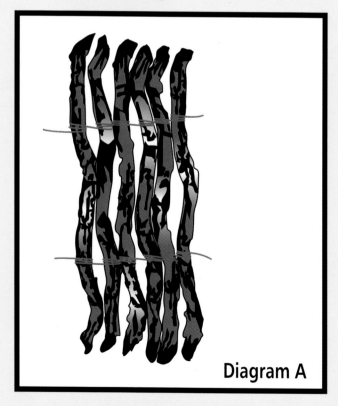

Diagram A

3
technique

Acrylic craft paint,
  mauve
Candles
Craft sticks
Découpage medium,
  matte finish
Disposable bowl
Disposable cup
Paintbrushes:
  ³/₄" flat soft-bristle;
  1" flat soft-bristle
Paper towels
Pet bird gravel (sand)

How do I add texture to paint using pet bird gravel or sand?

The elements of earth and fire are blended into today's decor with these highly textured candles. Fine sand, added sparingly to the painting medium, will enhance an oriental theme, while coarser sand can give that special retro-look of the '60s and '70s.

Sand-textured Candles

Here's How:

1. Texture the Candles

1. Prepare candles, following How do I prepare surfaces for faux finishing? Wax instructions on page 17.

2. Using a craft stick and a disposable bowl, mix approximately ⅓ cup pet bird gravel (sand) with water. Mix well and pour off excess water. Repeat until water runs clear.

3. Using your hand, scrape wet sand from bowl onto a pad of paper towels. Using a folded paper towel, pat sand to remove excess moisture.

4. Using a craft stick and a disposable cup, mix one part découpage medium with two parts mauve paint. Mix well.

5. Add one or two parts moistened sand to découpage medium/paint mixture, depending on amount of texture desired. Mix well.

   Note: There will be less chance for unsightly clumping if you use less sand and apply more coats. If sand has not adhered as tightly to wax surface as desired, apply one or two coats of diluted découpage medium over sand/paint.

6. Using a 1" soft-bristle paintbrush, apply texture to candles.

   Note: Avoid using an expensive paintbrush or a sponge brush as sand will actually cut the bristles or tear the sponge.

Design Tip: The texture of the sand, whether fine or coarse, dramatically effects the overall look of this technique.

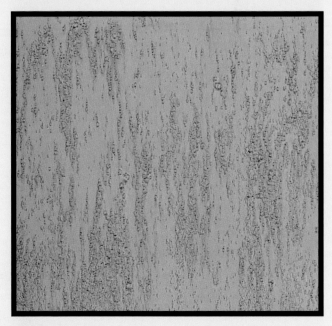

Any paint color can be used with the sand to achieve the same effect.

How do I cover the surfaces of an object using cement?

Complete your garden or that secret place by giving an authentic, aged look to a new piece of garden furniture. This easy and exciting technique can transform the ordinary with the magic of paint and patching cement.

What You Need To Get Started:

Acrylic craft paints:
   dark green;
   olive green;
   yellow ochre
Ceramic gargoyle
Concrete water-
   proofing sealer
Craft sticks
Découpage medium,
   matte finish
Dishwashing detergent
Disposable cups
Exterior varnish,
   satin finish
Newspaper
Paint scraper, narrow
Paintbrushes:
   1/2" flat stiff-bristle;
   1" flat China-bristle;
   #6 round soft-bristle
Paper towels
Patching cement
Plastic bucket
Plastic sheet
Rubbing alcohol
Stirring stick
Towel

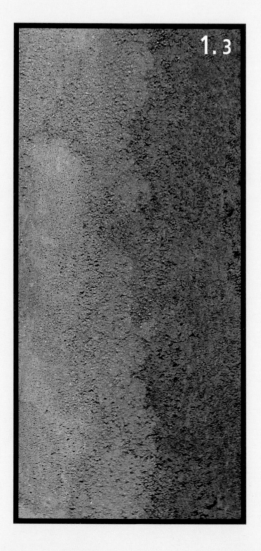

1.3

Cement-textured Gargoyle

Here's How:

1. Texture the Gargoyle

   1. Prepare gargoyle, following How do I prepare surfaces for faux finishing? Glass and Ceramic instructions on page 17.

   2. Using a stirring stick, mix one cup patching cement in a plastic bucket, following manufacturer's instructions.

   3. Using a 1" China-bristle paintbrush, bond-coat gargoyle by firmly brushing wet patching cement onto outer surfaces of gargoyle. Let dry for approximately two hours.

   4. Mix additional patching cement.

5. Using a ¹/₂" stiff-bristle paintbrush, apply wet patching cement onto outer surfaces of gargoyle, over bond coat.

   Note: If a smoother texture is desired, a paint scraper can be used on wet surface.

2. 4–5

6. Using a wet towel that has been wrung out, wrap gargoyle, then cover with a plastic sheet. Let dry and cure for 24 hours.

   Note: Do not expose to sunlight, heat, wind, rain, or frost during curing process.

7. Using concrete water-proofing sealer, seal cement-textured gargoyle, following manufacturer's instructions and warnings.

   Note: Do not pour any of the sealer down the drain. Pour any excess onto newspaper and dispose of in the garbage.

2. Apply the Weathered Patina Finish to the Gargoyle

   1. Using a craft stick and a disposable cup, mix two or three drops of yellow ochre paint with three tablespoons exterior varnish. Mix well.

   2. Using a 1" China-bristle paintbrush, apply a generous coat of paint/varnish mixture to gargoyle. Let dry for 24 hours.

   3. Using a craft stick and a disposable cup, mix dark green paint with water until mixture is thin and runs easily.

   4. Using a #6 soft-bristle paintbrush, apply dark green paint wash to gargoyle. Let dry.

   5. Using a craft stick and a disposable cup, mix two or three drops of olive green paint with three tablespoons exterior varnish. Mix well.

   6. Using a 1" China-bristle paintbrush, apply a generous coat of paint/varnish mixture to gargoyle. Let dry for 24 hours.

3. Seal the Gargoyle

   1. Using a 1" China-bristle paintbrush, apply a generous coat of exterior varnish to gargoyle to seal. Let dry for 24 hours.

**What You Need
To Get Started:**

Acrylic craft paints:
   lavender; light pink
Craft stick
Disposable cup
Mixing glaze, clear
Paintbrushes:
   1" flat China-bristle;
   1" flat soft-bristle
Primer
Rag, lint-free
Water-based varnish,
   satin finish
Wooden scrapbook
   cover, unfinished

How do I create a dimensional look using a lint-free rag?

A subtle design of soft, broken color is easy to achieve with today's specialized paints and glazing mediums. You add your own personal touch as you press the pattern onto your project.

31

Rag-rolled Scrapbook Cover

Here's How:

1. Paint the Scrapbook Cover

   1. Prepare scrapbook cover, following How do I prepare surfaces for faux finishing? Wood instructions on page 17.

   2. Using a 1" China-bristle paintbrush, apply a base coat of lavender paint to scrapbook cover. Let dry.

1.2

2. Rag-roll the Scrapbook Cover

   1. Using a craft stick and a disposable cup, mix three parts mixing glaze with one part light pink paint. Mix well.

   2. Using a 1" soft-bristle paintbrush, apply mixing glaze/paint mixture to scrapbook cover, over base coat.

   Note: Work quickly so mixing glaze/paint mixture does not dry on scrapbook cover. The next two steps require mixture to remain wet.

2.2

3. Thoroughly wet and wring out a lint-free rag. Loosely wad the rag into the palm of your hand and tuck in any loose ends.

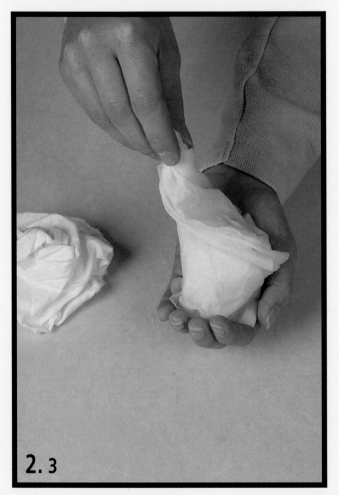

2. 3

Design Tip: This technique is a subtractive process. A portion of the layer of mixing glaze/paint mixture is being removed to expose the base-coat color. Different rag fabrics will render different looks.

4. Using gentle pressure, press rag over surface of wet scrapbook cover in a stamping motion. Lift and repeat several times. Rinse rag and repeat. Let dry thoroughly.

2. 4

3. Seal the Scrapbook Cover

1. Using a 1" China-bristle paintbrush, apply a generous coat of water-based varnish to scrapbook cover to seal. Let dry for 24 hours. Apply a second coat and let dry.

How do I create a textured look using a rubber combing tool?

Combing, an old folk-art technique, adds a clean, linear look to functional, as well as to decorative pieces. Yesterday's charm is at home in today's setting in a traditional blue and white color scheme.

**What You Need
To Get Started:**

Acrylic craft paint,
    light blue
Chest of drawers,
    unfinished
Craft stick
Disposable cup
Mixing glaze, clear
Paintbrush,
    2" flat China-bristle
Paper towels
Primer
Rubber combing tool
Satin-finish
    latex paint,
    bright white
Water-based varnish,
    satin finish

2. 2

Combed Chest of Drawers

Here's How:

1. Paint the Chest of Drawers

    1. Prepare chest of drawers, following How do I prepare surfaces for faux finishing? Wood instructions on page 17.

    2. Using a 2" China-bristle paintbrush, apply a base coat of bright white satin-finish latex paint to chest of drawers. Let dry for 24 hours.

2. Comb the Chest of Drawers

    1. Using a craft stick and a disposable cup, mix two parts mixing glaze with one part light blue acrylic craft paint. Mix well.

    2. Using a 2" China-bristle paintbrush, apply mixing glaze/paint mixture in long, vertical strokes, beginning at sides of chest.

    Note: Make certain to paint in the same direction as the combing will be done.

3. Using a rubber combing tool, pull tool through wet mixing glaze/paint mixture with even pressure.

   Note: To attain the proper look, hold the combing tool perpendicular to the surface.

2. 3

4. Using a paper towel, wipe combing tool at the end of each "swipe."

5. Repeat until all desired chest of drawer surfaces have been combed. Let dry for 24 hours.

3. Seal the Chest of Drawers

1. Using a 2" China-bristle paintbrush, apply a generous coat of water-based varnish to chest of drawers to seal. Let dry for 24 hours.

2. 5

Design Tip: Depending on the design of your project, it may be necessary to mask areas with masking tape. Use a "low-tack" painter's tape, then remove it immediately after mixing glaze/paint mixture has been applied. If there is spillover or the paint "bleeds" under the tape, remove with a damp cotton swab.

technique

**What You Need
To Get Started:**

Acrylic craft paints:
 bright blue; ivory
Corner shelf,
 unfinished
Crackle medium
Craft stick
Disposable cup
Paintbrushes:
 ³/₄" flat soft-bristle;
 1" flat China-bristle;
 1" flat soft-bristle
Paper towels
Primer
Water-based varnish,
 satin finish

How do I make a new object look weathered and aged?

Do you want to produce a mellow and worn look with new paint? The French invented the crackle glaze during the 18th century and it has never lost its popularity. Whether to reproduce a formal, fine crackle finish, or a bolder, casual country look, the choice is up to you.

Crackle-finished Corner Shelf

Here's How:

1. Paint the Corner Shelf

1. Prepare corner shelf, following How do I prepare surfaces for faux finishing? Wood instructions on page 17.

2. Using a ³/₄" soft-bristle paintbrush, apply a base coat of bright blue paint to corner shelf. Let dry.

1. 2

2. Crackle the Corner Shelf

1. Using a 1" China-bristle paintbrush, apply a coat of crackle medium to corner shelf, over base coat. Let dry until slightly tacky.

   Note: Use plenty of crackle medium. However, if it feels too thick or paintbrush feels like it is dragging, thin the next strokes with a few drops of water.

2. Using a craft stick and a disposable cup, slightly dilute ivory paint with water.

3. Using a 1" soft-bristle paintbrush, apply diluted acrylic craft paint over tacky surface of corner shelf. Let dry.

   Note: Work quickly, catching only the edge of the previous paintbrush stroke. Do not paint back into wet areas as it will lift the paint. As the corner shelf begins to dry, cracks will appear like magic! The thinner the application of diluted paint, the finer the cracks. The heavier the application of paint, the larger the cracks.

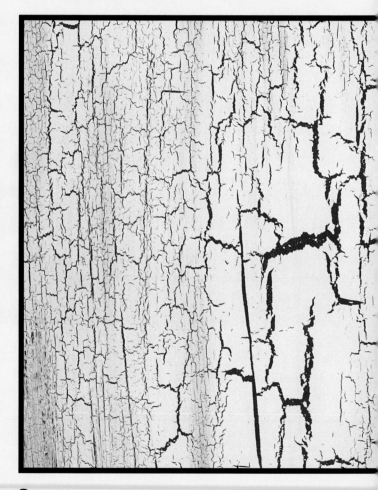

3. Seal the Corner Shelf

1. Using a 1" China-bristle paintbrush, apply a generous coat of water-based varnish to corner shelf to seal. Let dry for 24 hours. Apply a second coat and let dry.

technique

**What You Need
To Get Started:**

Acrylic craft paints:
  black; bronze;
  reddish brown;
  light olive green;
  reddish purple;
  dusty sage;
  dusty violet
Ceramic lamp
Cheesecloth
Craft sticks
Découpage medium,
  matte finish
Dishwashing detergent
Disposable cups
Mixing glaze, clear
Newspaper
Paintbrushes:
  $1/4$" flat stiff-bristle;
  1" flat China-bristle;
  #8 round soft-bristle;
  #8 scumbling
Paper towels
Rubbing alcohol
Water-based
  spray varnish,
  matte finish

How do I make a new object look like an antique?

A gradual build-up of translucent layers of paint gives depth and a time-worn quality to detailed surfaces. Dark glazes worked into recessed areas accent the subtle colors of raised patterns.

Antiqued Lamp

Here's How:

1. Paint the Lamp

1. Prepare lamp, following How do I prepare surfaces for faux finishing? Glass and Ceramic instructions on page 17.

2. Using a craft stick and a disposable cup, mix two parts mixing glaze with one part black and one part bronze paints. Mix well.

3. Using a #8 soft-bristle paintbrush, apply a coat of mixing glaze/paint mixture to background of lamp. Let dry.

4. Using a craft stick and a disposable cup, mix equal parts of mixing glaze and dusty violet paint. Mix well.

5. Using a #8 soft-bristle paintbrush, apply a coat of mixing glaze/paint mixture to grapes on lamp. Let dry.

6. Using a craft stick and a disposable cup, mix equal parts of mixing glaze and reddish purple paint. Mix well.

7. Using a #8 soft-bristle paintbrush, apply a coat of mixing glaze/paint mixture to a few of the grapes on lamp. Let dry.

8. Using a craft stick and a disposable cup, mix equal parts of mixing glaze and dusty sage paint. Mix well.

9. Using a #8 soft-bristle paintbrush, apply a coat of mixing glaze/paint mixture to grape stems and leaves on lamp. Let dry.

10. Using a craft stick and a disposable cup, mix equal parts of mixing glaze and light olive green paint. Mix well.

11. Using a #8 soft-bristle paintbrush, apply a coat of mixing glaze/paint mixture to a few of the grape stems and leaves on lamp. Let dry.

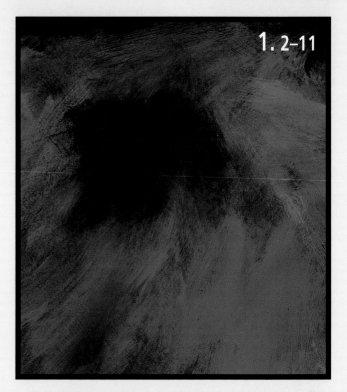

1. 2–11

12. Using a #8 scumbling paintbrush, work mixing glaze/black and bronze paint mixture into all crevices and detailed areas.

13. Using a 1" China-bristle paintbrush, whisk paint from raised surfaces. Let dry.

Note: Repeat applications of paint for more depth of color.

2. Antique the Lamp

1. Using a craft stick and a disposable cup, mix three parts mixing glaze with one part black and one part reddish brown paints. Mix well.

2. Using a 1" China-bristle paintbrush, apply mixing glaze/paint mixture (antiquing glaze) over surfaces of lamp.

3. Using cheesecloth, gently buff paint from high points of surfaces.

Note: If a heavier antique finish is desired, allow antiquing glaze to dry and apply a second coat.

2. 2–3

3. Spatter the Lamp

1. Slightly dilute black paint with water.

2. Load a ¼" stiff-bristle paintbrush with diluted black paint.

3. Refer back to the following steps on page 22 for Technique 1: Spatter the Bowl, Steps 1 and 4 (includes photograph).

4. Repeat with diluted bronze paint. Let dry.

4. Seal the Lamp

1. Using water-based spray varnish, apply a light, even coat to lamp to seal. Let dry. Apply two additional coats and let dry after each application.

3. 3–4

How do I apply paint to a surface or object using a sponge?

The softness and random patterning created by using a natural sea sponge works beautifully on many surfaces. The texture on this aquarium stand is blended even more by using a softening brush to smooth wet glaze and paint.

**What You Need
To Get Started:**

Acrylic craft paints:
   dark blue-green;
   medium blue-green;
   burnt sienna;
   burnt umber
Aquarium with stand,
   unfinished
Craft sticks
Disposable plates
Mixing glazes:
   clear; mocha; pewter
Natural sea sponge
Newspaper
Paintbrushes:
   ³/₄" flat soft-bristle;
   1" flat China-bristle;
   softening
Primer
Satin-finish latex paint,
   beige
Solvent-based varnish,
   high-gloss finish

Sponge-painted Aquarium Stand

Here's How:

1. Paint the Stand

   1. Prepare aquarium stand, following How do I prepare surfaces for faux finishing? Wood instructions on page 17.

   2. Using a ³/₄" soft-bristle paintbrush, apply a base coat of beige satin-finish latex paint to stand. Let dry.

2. Sponge-paint the Stand

   1. Using a craft stick and a disposable plate, mix two parts clear mixing glaze with one part burnt sienna paint. Mix well.

   2. Thoroughly wet and wring out a natural sea sponge.

   3. Dip wet sea sponge into mixing glaze/paint mixture, then lightly blot off excess onto newspaper.

4. Using gentle pressure, press sea sponge over surface of stand in a random pattern, slightly rotating your hand each time. Lift and repeat several times. Rinse sea sponge and repeat.

   Note: Overlap rotations so they blend into a natural-looking pattern.

5. Using a softening paintbrush and a light sweeping motion, soften sponge-painted areas while mixing glaze/paint mixture is still wet.

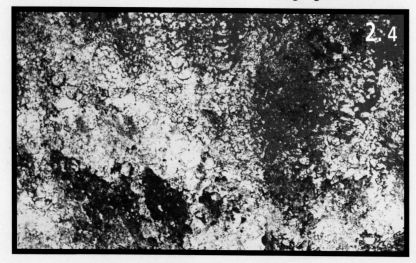

6. Using a craft stick and a disposable plate, mix two parts clear mixing glaze with one part burnt umber paint. Mix well.

7. Sponge-paint surface of stand, over previous pattern.

8. Using a softening paintbrush, soften sponge-painted areas while mixing glaze/paint mixture is still wet.

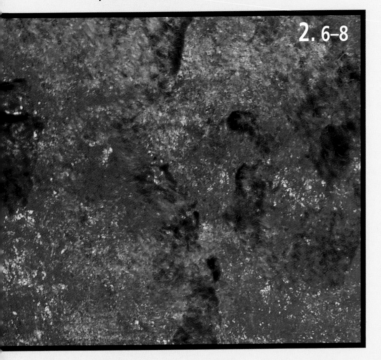

2. 6–8

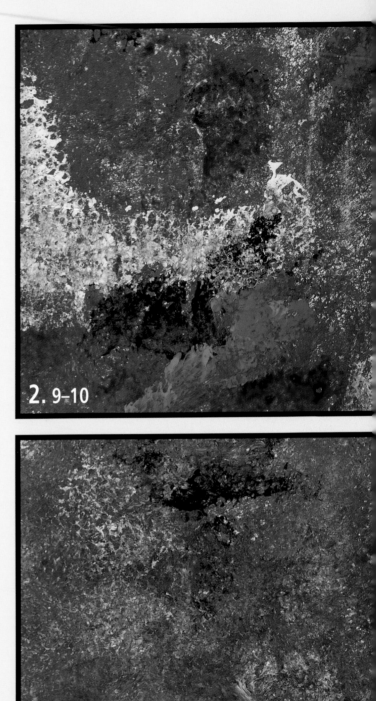

2. 9–10

2. 11

9. Sponge-paint small areas of stand with mocha mixing glaze. Repeat with pewter mixing glaze.

10. Sponge-paint small areas of stand with medium blue-green paint. Repeat with dark blue-green paint. Repeat with beige satin-finish latex paint.

11. Using a softening paintbrush, soften sponge-painted areas while mixing glazes and paints are still wet. Let dry.

3. Seal the Stand

1. Using a 1" China-bristle paintbrush, apply a generous coat of solvent-based varnish to stand to seal. Let dry for 24 hours. Apply a second coat and let dry.

10
technique

**What You Need
To Get Started:**

Acrylic craft paints:
    metallic gold;
    black-green;
    dark forest green;
    green; medium
    blue-green;
    opalescent;
    dark tan; light tan;
    antique white
Craft sticks
Disposable cups
Mixing glaze, clear
Paintbrushes:
    #2 round soft-bristle;
    #6 round soft-bristle;
    #8 scumbling
Paper towels
Primer
Tinting medium,
    iridescent
Water-based varnish,
    satin finish
Wooden candleholder,
    unfinished

How do I blend colors
by stippling?

A fine, mottled surface adds a timeless quality to
these candleholders. Deep, jewel-toned colors blend easily
into soft pastels. This technique adds life to small pieces,
but is equally attractive applied to large areas.

45

Dark Green Stippled Candleholder

Here's How:

1. Stipple the Candleholder

    1. Prepare candleholder, following How do I prepare surfaces for faux finishing? Wood instructions on page 17.

    2. Using craft sticks and disposable cups, mix one part mixing glaze with two parts paint for each of the following colors: black-green, dark forest green, dark tan, light tan, and antique white.

    3. Using a craft stick and a disposable cup, mix two parts mixing glaze with one part medium blue-green paint.

    4. Using a #8 scumbling paintbrush, and beginning at base of candleholder, stipple mixing glaze/black-green paint mixture. Using a light, quick pouncing motion, tap the color onto candleholder in a random pattern. Change directions often.

    5. Continue stippling up the candleholder, using mixing glaze/dark forest green paint mixture.

        Note: To make a subtle transition between colors, pounce color mixtures into each other. Do not use water.

    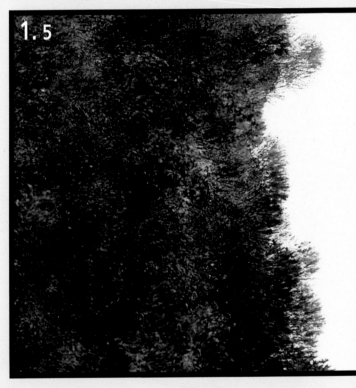

    1.5

    6. At the center of candleholder, stipple mixing glaze/medium blue-green paint mixture.

    7. Continue stippling up the candleholder, using mixing glaze/dark tan paint mixture.

1.4

Design Tip: If you wish to lighten an area, dip the tip of the paintbrush into clear mixing glaze and stipple over the painted areas.

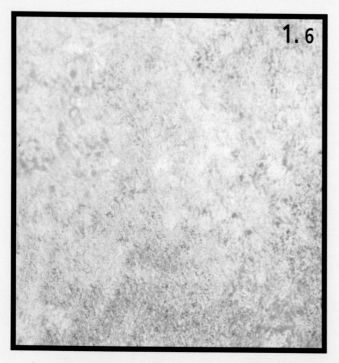

1. 6

8. Continue stippling up the candleholder, using mixing glaze/light tan paint mixture.

9. At top of candleholder, stipple mixing glaze/antique white paint mixture. Let dry.

10. Using a craft stick and a disposable cup, mix one part mixing glaze with two parts metallic gold paint.

11. Using a #2 soft-bristle paintbrush, stipple mixing glaze/metallic gold paint mixture onto desired areas. Let dry.

12. Using a #6 soft-bristle paintbrush, apply a coat of iridescent tinting medium to add a pearl sheen to candleholder. Let dry.

2. Seal the Candleholder

  1. Using a #6 soft-bristle paintbrush, apply a generous coat of water-based varnish to candleholder to seal. Let dry for 24 hours.

1. 11–12

Burgundy Stippled Candleholder

Repeat steps provided for dark green stippled candleholder, substituting the following acrylic craft paint colors:

green .... burgundy

black-green .... black-burgundy

dark forest .... deep blue-red

medium blue-green .... medium crimson

11
technique

Acrylic craft paints:
  metallic gold;
  metallic pewter;
  light yellow cream
Chalk pencil
Cloth, lint-free
Disposable plate
Paintbrush,
  2" flat China-bristle
Plastic scouring pad
Primer
Stencil, diamond
Stencil spray adhesive
Water-based
  spray varnish,
  satin finish
Wedge-shaped
  cosmetic sponges
Wooden table,
  unfinished

How do I stencil on fine furnishings?

Stenciling, a centuries-old technique, gives new life and interest to furnishings long past their prime. Designs may be simple or complex, subtle or glamorous. A diamond-shaped pattern and touches of gold add distinction to this dining area.

Stenciled Tabletop

Here's How:

1. Paint the Table

1. Prepare table, following How do I prepare surfaces for faux finishing? Wood instructions on page 17.

2. Using a 2" China-bristle paintbrush, apply a base coat of light yellow cream paint to table. Let dry for 24 hours.

2. Stencil the Tabletop

1. Using a stencil and a chalk pencil, determine pattern placement on tabletop and lightly mark.

    Note: Make certain to use a light shade chalk pencil so it won't show through the application of paint. Otherwise, the markings need to be removed prior to applying paint.

2. Spray stencil with stencil spray adhesive, following manufacturer's instructions.

    Note: Stencil spray adhesive provides a light tack which will keep stencil from slipping as you work. It also keeps the paint from "bleeding" under the openings of the stencil.

3. Place approximately one teaspoon metallic gold and metallic pewter paints onto a disposable plate. Do not mix.

4. Using a wedge-shaped cosmetic sponge, gently tap the short, flat end into metallic gold paint and apply to left side of diamond openings in stencil.

5. Using another wedge-shaped cosmetic sponge, repeat with metallic pewter paint on right side of diamond openings.

6. Carefully lift stencil from tabletop. Let dry. Repeat until pattern is complete. Let dry for 24 hours.

7. Using a plastic scouring pad, lightly buff tabletop.

8. Using a cloth, wipe tabletop to remove excess dust.

3. Seal the Table

1. Using water-based spray varnish, apply a light, even coat to tabletop to seal. Let dry. Apply two additional coats and let dry after each application.

2. 4–5

2. 6

12
technique

What You Need To Get Started:

Acrylic craft paint:
  deep blue-green
Craft stick
Dishwashing detergent
Disposable cups
Footstool, unfinished
Malt vinegar
Paintbrushes:
  1" flat China-bristle;
  1" flat soft-bristle;
  2" flat China-bristle;
  #8 scumbling;
  #10 round soft-bristle
Plastic scouring pad
Plastic squeeze bottle,
  16 ounce
Powder pigment,
  copper
Primer
Solvent-based varnish,
  gloss finish
Sugar
Tack cloth
Water-based varnish,
  gloss finish

How do I use household vinegar as a paint additive?

The origins of vinegar painting have been lost. However, this humble technique is enjoying a renewed interest. Popular on furniture and decorative accessories, few mediums allow the artist so much creativity with visual effects.

Vinegar-painted Footstool

Here's How:

1. Paint the Footstool

1. Prepare footstool, following How do I prepare surfaces for faux finishing? Wood instructions on page 17.

2. Using a craft stick and a disposable cup, mix deep blue-green paint with a few drops of water-based varnish.

    Note: The consistency of this paint/varnish mixture should be that of medium cream.

3. Using a 2" China-bristle paintbrush, apply a coat of paint/varnish mixture to footstool. Let dry for 24 hours. Apply a second coat and let dry.

2. Vinegar-paint the Footstool

1. Using a plastic squeeze bottle, mix two teaspoons sugar and 1/4 teaspoon dish-washing detergent with one pint malt vinegar.

2. Measure one teaspoon copper powder pigment into a disposable cup.

3. Add one teaspoon detergent/vinegar mixture to powder pigment. Using a #10 soft-bristle paintbrush, mix well.

4. Add one more teaspoon detergent/vinegar mixture and stir vigorously. Continue adding detergent/vinegar mixture until vinegar paint is almost runny.

    Note: Bubbles should appear, but vinegar paint should not be frothy. This stirring process must be repeated before each application.

5. Using a 1" soft-bristle paintbrush, apply vinegar paint to one side of footstool.

    Note: Brush marks will be visible in the paint, but the surface should be covered well.

3. Stipple the Footstool

1. Refer back to the following step on page 46 for Technique 10: Stipple the Candleholder, Step 4 (includes photograph).

   Note: Do not apply additional vinegar paint. Simply stipple wet vinegar paint to blend. Let dry.

2. Using a 1" soft-bristle paintbrush, apply vinegar paint to another side of footstool. Stipple this side. Let dry.

   Note: Repeat vinegar paint application and stippling for each side.

4. Seal the Footstool

1. Using a 1" China-bristle paintbrush, gently apply a light coat of solvent-based varnish to footstool to seal. Let dry.

   Note: Solvent-based varnish must be used for this technique because the moisture in water-based varnish will dissolve the vinegar paint.

2. Using a plastic scouring pad, lightly buff footstool.

3. Using a tack cloth, wipe footstool to remove excess dust.

4. Apply a second coat of varnish. Let dry.

3. 1–2

How do I rust a nonmetal surface using a rusting agent?

Giving the look of rusted metal to a variety of surfaces is as easy as applying a coat of paint. Equally at home, indoors or out, this rusted patina is created with a paint made from ground iron particles, and then brushing on a rusting solution.

What You Need To Get Started:

Acrylic craft paints:
   metallic gold;
   blue-green;
   metallic pewter;
   rust; white
Ceramic bird
   on a steel post
Craft sticks
Découpage medium,
   matte finish
Dishwashing detergent
Disposable cup
Disposable plate
Eyedropper
Newspaper
Paintbrush,
   1" flat China-bristle
Paper towels
Rubbing alcohol
Rusting agent,
   two-step
Sand, extra-fine
Sandpaper,
   medium-grit
Terra-cotta pots

Rusted Pots and Bird

Here's How:

1. Texture the Pots and Bird

    1. Prepare pots and bird, following How do I prepare surfaces for faux finishing? Glass and Ceramic instructions on page 17.

    2. Using a craft stick and a disposable cup, mix ¼ cup sand, one tablespoon découpage medium, and two tablespoons white paint. Mix well.

    3. Using a 1" China-bristle paintbrush, apply one coat of sand/découpage medium/paint mixture to the surfaces to be rusted. Let dry.

2. Paint the Pots and Bird

    1. Using a craft stick and a disposable plate, mix equal parts of metallic gold and metallic pewter paints. Mix well.

    2. Using a 1" China-bristle paintbrush, and working vertically, apply metallic paint mixture over textured surface.

    3. Apply streaks of blue-green and rust paints over metallic paint, before it has had a chance to dry. Let dry.

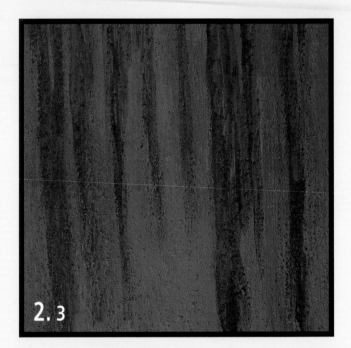

2. 3

3. Rust the Pots and Bird

    1. Using newspaper, cover work surface to protect it from runs and drips.

    2. Apply a two-step rusting agent to pots and bird, following manufacturer's instructions. Let dry for 24 hours.

        Note: An eyedropper is ideal for applying the second step of liquid activator.

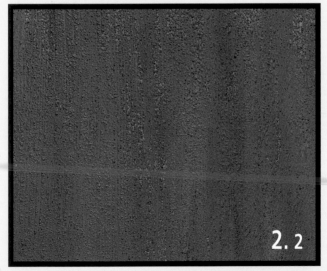

2. 2

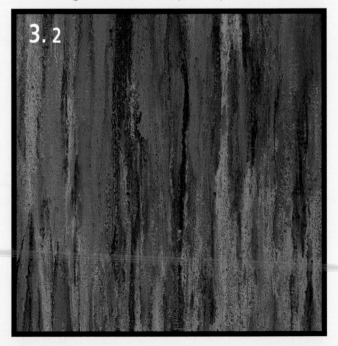

3. 2

**What You Need
To Get Started:**

Acrylic craft paints:
  black; dark gray-blue;
  dark brown;
  metallic gold;
  sage green
Cheesecloth
Craft sticks
Disposable cups
Disposable plates
Gourds
Mixing glaze, clear
Newspaper
Paintbrushes:
  3/4" flat soft-bristle;
  1" flat China-bristle;
  #8 scumbling;
  softening
Primer
Sponges, synthetic
Water-based varnish,
  satin finish

How do I achieve the look of bronze using paint?

Artifacts from the bronze age? Not really. These dried gourds, whether from the market or from your garden, provide an intriguing accent to a shelf or table arrangement. This easy bronzing technique adds a touch of distinction to the ordinary.

Bronzed Gourds

Here's How:

1. Paint the Gourds

    1. Prepare gourds, following How do I pre-
    pare surfaces for faux finishing? Wood
    instructions on page 17.

    2. Using a ³⁄₄" soft-bristle paintbrush, apply
    a base coat of metallic gold paint to
    gourds. Let dry. Apply a second coat
    and let dry.

    3. Using craft sticks and disposable cups,
    mix four parts mixing glaze with one
    part dark brown paint; mix three parts
    mixing glaze with one part dark gray-
    blue paint; and mix two parts mixing
    glaze with one part sage green paint.

    4. Using a 1" China-bristle paintbrush, apply
    mixing glaze/paint mixtures to gourds.

1. 2

1. 4

2. Stipple the Gourds

1. Refer back to the following step on page 46 for Technique 10: Stipple the Candleholder, Step 4 (includes photograph).

   Note: Do not apply additional mixing glaze/paint. Simply stipple wet mixing glaze/paint mixtures to blend. If necessary, more mixing glaze/paint can be applied. Let dry until slightly tacky.

3. Sponge-paint the Gourds

1. Using a craft stick and a disposable plate, mix two parts mixing glaze with one part black paint. Mix well.

2. Thoroughly wet and wring out a synthetic sponge.

3. Refer back to the following steps on page 43 for Technique 9: Sponge-paint the Stand, Steps 3–5.

   Note: This process will deposit some mixing glaze/black paint mixture and lift some of the tacky paint.

4. Using a dry synthetic sponge, lightly sponge-paint a small amount of mixing glaze randomly into areas of mixing glaze/black paint. Let dry until slightly tacky.

5. Fold a piece of cheesecloth into a pad and gently rub surface of gourds to blend colors. Let dry.

4. Seal the Gourds

1. Using a 1" China-bristle paintbrush, apply a generous coat of water-based varnish to gourds to seal. Let dry for 24 hours. Apply a second coat and let dry.

Design Tip: If you wish to add a green cast to the bronzing, repeat sponge-painting instructions with sage green and dark blue paints.

How do I apply gilding leaf to a surface or object?

Traditional gilding takes great patience and is extremely time consuming. This process, which I call broken gilding, is simple and effective as a decorative technique. It gives a convincing feel of the antique with instant results.

**What You Need
To Get Started:**

Carved wooden charger,
   unfinished
Cheesecloth
Cloth, lint-free
Finishing wax
Gilding adhesive
Gilding leaf
Paintbrushes:
   $^1/_2$" flat soft-bristle;
   $^3/_4$" flat soft-bristle;
   #4 round soft-bristle
Primer
Rubbing alcohol
Water-based varnish,
   satin finish

1. 2

Gilded Charger

Here's How:

1. Apply the Gilding
   to the Carved Charger

   1. Prepare carved charger, following How do I prepare surfaces for faux finishing? Wood instructions on page 17.

   2. Using a $^3/_4$" soft-bristle paintbrush, apply two coats of gilding adhesive to random areas of the charger where the gilding leaf is to be applied. Let dry until slightly tacky.

   3. Using a #4 soft-bristle paintbrush, work gilding adhesive into recessed areas of carved surfaces on charger. Let dry until slightly tacky.

4. Pick up a piece of gilding leaf which has gently been removed from its packaging, and lay over the area where tacky gilding adhesive has been applied.

   Note: Cover only one to two square inches at a time.

5. Using a ½" soft-bristle paintbrush, gently push gilding leaf into recessed areas where gilding adhesive has been applied.

   Note: Because the paintbrush will pick up gilding adhesive and bits of gilding leaf as you work, occasionally it will be necessary to rinse the paintbrush with rubbing alcohol. Make certain to wipe paintbrush dry before proceeding.

1. 5

1. 4

6. Continue adding gilding leaf until application is complete.

7. Fold a piece of cheesecloth into a pad and dampen with rubbing alcohol, then gently rub over gilded areas.

   Note: This will help remove "imperfections" and loose gilding leaf from the surface.

8. Repeat with a folded piece of cheese cloth dampened with water.

2. Seal the Carved Charger

1. Using a ³/₄" soft-bristle paintbrush, apply a generous coat of water-based varnish to gilded areas on carved charger to seal. Let dry for 24 hours. Apply a second coat and let dry.

2. Using a lint-free cloth and finishing wax, rub all remaining unfinished wood, then lightly buff.

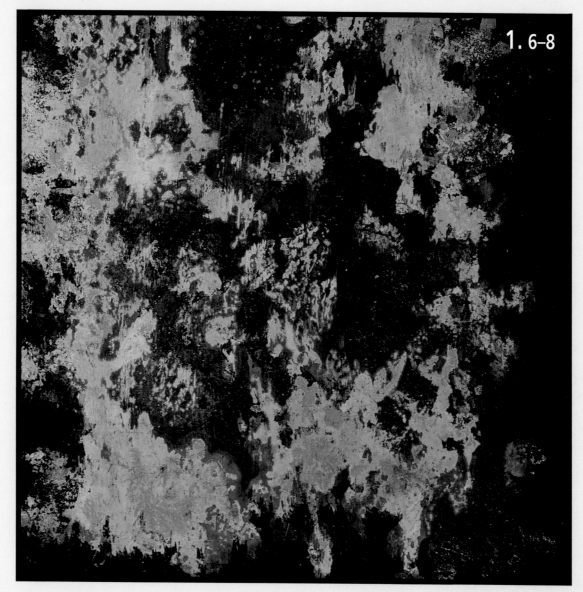

1. 6–8

How do I achieve the look of distressed wood using paint and wax?

Add charm and interest to your surface with the vintage look of peeled and chipped paint. No more scraping and heavy sanding are necessary with this treatment. Want more flair? Try using nontraditional colors.

1.4

What You Need To Get Started:

Acrylic craft paints:
    medium dusty blue;
    burgundy; orange;
    dusty rose
Candle wax
Craft stick
Disposable cup
Disposable plate
Hairdryer
Natural sea sponge
Paintbrush,
    1" flat China-bristle
Paper towels
Plastic scouring pad
Primer
Rubber cement
Water-based varnish,
    gloss finish
Wooden frame,
    unfinished

Distressed Frame

Here's How:

1. Paint and Distress the Frame

   1. Prepare frame, following How do I prepare surfaces for faux finishing? Wood instructions on page 17.

   2. Using a craft stick and a disposable cup, mix two drops of burgundy and one drop of orange paints with $1/4$ cup water-based varnish. Mix well.

   3. Using a 1" China-bristle paintbrush, apply a light coat of paint/varnish mixture to frame. Let dry. Apply a second coat and let dry.

   4. Using candle wax, rub outer surface of frame in a random pattern, working with grain of wood.

5. Using a small piece of dampened natural sea sponge, apply rubber cement over waxed frame in a random pattern. Let dry for 24 hours.

6. Using a 1" China-bristle paintbrush, apply a base coat of medium dusty blue paint to frame. Let dry.

7. Apply a second coat of rubber cement over painted frame in a random pattern. Let dry for 24 hours.

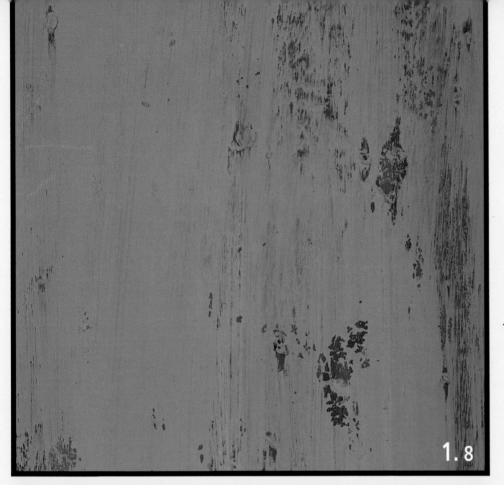

1.8

8. Using a 1" China-bristle paintbrush, apply a base coat of dusty rose paint to frame. Let dry.

9. Using a plastic scouring pad, buff frame to remove some paint, rubber cement, and wax.

10. Using a hairdryer and paper towels, apply heat and buff frame.

1.9–10

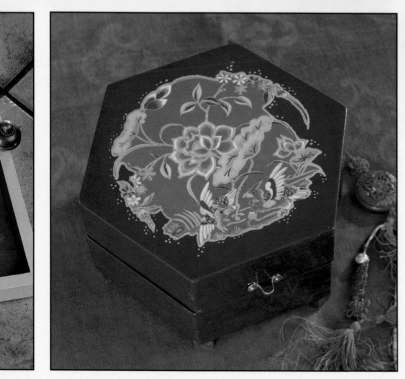

Section 3:
*techniques
beyond
the basics*

17

technique

What You Need To Get Started:

Acrylic craft paints:
   black; bright blue;
   gold; deep blue-
   green
Craft sticks
Disposable cups
Mixing glaze, clear
Natural sea sponges
Newspaper
Paintbrushes:
   ¹/₄" flat soft-bristle;
   ¹/₄" flat stiff-bristle;
   ³/₄" flat soft-bristle;
   #8 scumbling;
   softening
Primer
Sandpaper,
   ultrafine
Tack cloth
Water-based varnish,
   gloss finish
Wooden box with
   removable lid,
   unfinished

How do I create a finish using paintbrushes and sponges?

Strong color and a "deep" surface give this small box weight and substance. The look of polished stone is accomplished by layering brilliant colors, blending with paintbrushes and sponges, and layering more colors. This simple process creates a distinctive look.

Lapis-finished Box

Here's How:

1. Paint the Box and Lid

   1. Prepare box and lid, following How do I prepare surfaces for faux finishing? Wood instructions on page 17.

   2. Using craft sticks and disposable cups, mix one part mixing glaze with one part paint for each of the following colors: black, bright blue, and deep blue-green. Mix well.

   3. Using a ³/₄" soft-bristle paintbrush, apply mixing glaze/paint mixtures to areas of wooden box and lid in a random pattern.

1.4

1.3

   4. Using a clean, dry ¹/₄" soft-bristle paintbrush, smooth wet glazed/painted surfaces and slightly blend colors.

2. Sponge-paint the Box and Lid

   1. Refer back to the following steps on page 43 for Technique 9: Sponge-paint the Stand, Steps 2, 4, and 5.

      Note: Do not apply additional mixing glaze/paint. Simply sponge-paint wet mixing glaze/paint mixtures to blend.

   2. Using another small piece of dampened sea sponge, drag over wet mixing glaze/paint to remove some paint and create white streaks. Let dry.

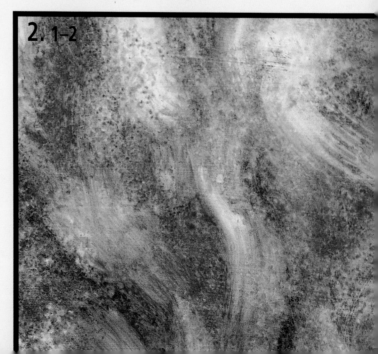

2.1–2

3. Stipple the Box and Lid

1. Using a craft stick and a disposable cup, mix one part mixing glaze with one part bright blue paint. Mix well.

2. Refer back to the following step on page 46 for Technique 10: Stipple the Candleholder, Step 4 (includes photograph).

   Note: Stipple next to the white streaks.

3. Using a natural sea sponge, soften and blend bright blue paint edges. Let dry.

   Note: It may be necessary to "roll" the sponge in paper towels to remove excess paint.

4. Add Additional Paint and Pattern to the Box and Lid

1. Using craft sticks and disposable cups, mix three parts mixing glaze with one part paint for each of the following colors: bright blue, burgundy, and deep blue-green.

2. Using a dampened natural sea sponge, sponge over wet mixing glaze/paint to blend colors.

   Note: This glaze/paint application should enhance the previous patterns created and should not cover them up.

3. Using a clean, dry ¼" soft-bristle paintbrush, smooth wet glazed/painted surfaces and slightly blend colors. Let dry.

   Note: If there are any tiny imperfections in the glazed/painted surfaces, they can be removed before sealing.

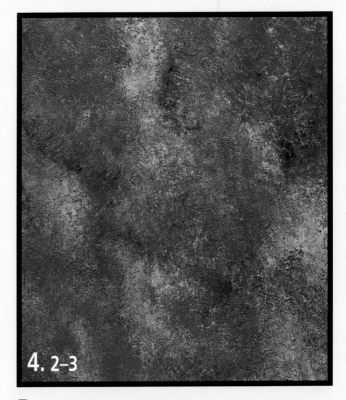

5. Seal the Box and Lid

1. Using a ³/₄" soft-bristle paintbrush, apply a generous coat of water-based varnish to box and lid to seal. Let dry. Apply a second coat and let dry.

   Note: Using ultrafine sandpaper, sand surfaces between each application of varnish. Using a tack cloth, wipe box and lid to remove excess dust.

6. Spatter the Box and Lid

1. Slightly dilute gold paint with water.

2. Load a ¼" stiff-bristle paintbrush with diluted gold paint.

3. Refer back to the following steps on page 22 for Technique 1: Spatter the Bowl, Steps 1 and 4 (includes photograph).

7. Reseal the Box and Lid

1. Using a ¾" soft-bristle paintbrush, apply a generous coat of water-based varnish to box and lid to seal. Let dry. Apply a second coat and let dry.

6.3

7.1

Design Tip: The inside of this box and lid were finished with small pieces of gift wrap, torn and glued. Seal with varnish.

71

18
technique

**What You Need
To Get Started:**

Acrylic craft paints:
  deep navy blue;
  metallic gold
Cloth, lint-free
Color copy
Craft sticks
Découpage medium,
  matte finish
Disposable cups
Gesso
Paintbrushes:
  1" flat China-bristle;
  1" flat soft-bristle;
  #0 liner
Primer
Sandpaper,
  fine
Scissors
Tack cloth
Water-based varnish,
  elite diamond finish
Wooden box with
  removable lid,
  unfinished

How do I create a high-gloss finish using a dampened cloth and a paintbrush?

The Chinese are credited with inventing the smooth, highly polished surface known as lacquer. This multi-layering process is accomplished with surprising ease by using modern finishes. A color copy of a traditional Chinese design adds an authentic touch to this oriental theme.

Lacquered Box

Here's How:

1. Prepare the Box and Lid

1. Prepare box and lid, following How do I prepare surfaces for faux finishing? Wood instructions on page 17.

2. Using a craft stick and a disposable cup, mix gesso with a few drops of water-based varnish.

   Note: The consistency of this gesso/varnish mixture should be that of medium cream.

3. Using a 1" China-bristle paintbrush, apply a coat of gesso/varnish mixture to box and lid. Let dry.

4. Using sandpaper, sand inner and outer surfaces of box and lid.

5. Using a tack cloth, wipe box and lid to remove excess dust.

6. Apply a second coat of gesso/varnish mixture to box and lid. Let dry.

7. Using sandpaper and a tack cloth, sand box and lid a second time and wipe to remove excess dust.

2. Paint the Box and Lid

1. Using a 1" China-bristle paintbrush, apply a base coat of deep navy blue paint to box and lid. Let dry. Apply a second coat and let dry.

2.1

3. Apply the Decorative Image
to the Box and Lid

1. Using scissors, cut out an image from a color copy as desired.

2. Using a craft stick and a disposable cup, mix one part découpage medium with one part water. Mix well.

3. Using a 1" soft-bristle paintbrush, apply diluted découpage medium to top side of box lid. Let dry.

4. Position image on lid as desired.

5. Using a slightly dampened cloth, gently rub image from center of the design to outside edges. Let dry for 24 hours.

   Note: Make certain to work out all air bubbles and clean up all traces of découpage medium. If a bubble appears, prick it with a straight pin and using a finger and dampened cloth, gently press. Do not rub.

3. 3–5

6. Using a craft stick and a disposable cup, mix metallic gold paint with a few drops of water.

   Note: The consistency of this diluted paint should be that of medium cream.

7. Using a #0 liner paintbrush, outline edges of decorative image. Add clusters of dots as desired.

4. 1

4. Seal the Box and Lid

1. Using a 1" soft-bristle paintbrush, apply a generous coat of water-based varnish to box and lid to seal. Let dry. To achieve a high-gloss finish, apply five additional coats and let dry after each application.

   Note: Some varnishes are very thin and tend to bead at the edges of boxes and box lids and have a tendency to run down the sides. If this happens, immediately brush out these problem areas.

Design Tip: The inside of this box and lid were finished with small pieces of gift wrap, torn and glued. Seal with varnish.

technique

**What You Need
To Get Started:**

Acrylic craft paints:
  black; medium gray;
  metallic pewter;
  white
Craft sticks
Découpage medium,
  matte finish
Dishwashing detergent
Disposable cups
Disposable plates
Metal vase
Mixing glaze, clear
Natural sea sponge
Newspaper
Paintbrushes:
  1/4" flat stiff-bristle;
  3/4" flat soft-bristle;
  3/4" flat stiff-bristle;
  1" flat China-bristle;
  softening
Paper towels
Rubbing alcohol
Sandpaper,
  medium-grit
Water-based varnish,
  satin finish

How do I achieve the look of stone using paint?

There are many colors and variations found in granite. However, all types of this rock have similarities due to their speckled appearance. To provide an effect with the weight and character of this stone, simple spattering and sponge-painting are the chosen techniques.

Granite-look Vase

Here's How:

1. Paint the Vase

1. Prepare vase, following How do I prepare surfaces for faux finishing? Metal instructions on page 17.

2. Using a ³/₄" soft-bristle paintbrush, apply a base coat of medium gray paint to vase. Let dry.

2. 3

1. 2

4. Using a craft stick and a disposable plate, mix three parts mixing glaze with two parts medium gray and one part white paints.

5. Sponge-paint vase, over mixing glaze/black paint sponged areas.

6. Add one or two additional drops of white paint to mixing glaze/medium gray and white paint mixture.

7. Sponge-paint vase, over mixing glaze/medium gray and white paint sponged areas. Let dry.

2. Sponge-paint the Vase

1. Using a craft stick and a disposable plate, mix two parts mixing glaze with one part black paint. Mix well.

2. Thoroughly wet and wring out a natural sea sponge.

3. Refer back to the following steps on page 43 for Technique 9: Sponge-paint the Stand, Steps 3–5.

2. 4–7

3. Spatter the Vase

1. Slightly dilute white paint with water.

2. Load a ¼" stiff-bristle paintbrush with diluted white paint.

3. Refer back to the following steps on page 22 for Technique 1: Spatter the Bowl, Steps 1 and 4 (includes photograph).

4. Repeat with diluted metallic pewter paint. Let dry.

5. Repeat with diluted black paint. Let dry.

4. Seal the Vase

1. Using a 1" China-bristle paintbrush, apply a generous coat of water-based varnish to vase to seal. Let dry for 24 hours. Apply a second coat and let dry.

3. 3–5

4. 1

How do I create a textured look using tissue paper?

Frottage, from the French, literally means to rub. Wrapping tissue paper, pressed into a glaze of transparent color, then removed, leaves a cloud-like impression, which is the essence of this elegant technique.

What You Need To Get Started:

Acrylic craft paints:
   deep burgundy;
   gold
Ceramic ginger jar
Cloth, lint-free
Craft sticks
Découpage medium,
   matte finish
Dishwashing detergent
Disposable cups
Mixing glaze, clear
Paintbrushes:
   1" flat China-bristle;
   1" flat soft-bristle;
   softening
Paper towels
Rubbing alcohol
Tissue paper
Water-based varnish,
   elite diamond finish

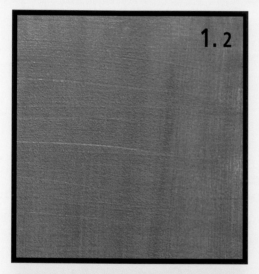

1.2

1.4

Frottaged Ginger Jar

Here's How:

1. Paint the Ginger Jar

   1. Prepare ginger jar, following How do I prepare surfaces for faux finishing? Glass and Ceramic instructions on page 17.

   2. Using a 1" soft-bristle paintbrush, apply a base coat of gold paint to ginger jar. Let dry. Apply a second coat and let dry.

   3. Using a craft stick and a disposable cup, mix three parts mixing glaze with one part deep burgundy paint. Mix well.

   4. Using a 1" soft-bristle paintbrush, apply mixing glaze/paint mixture to ginger jar, over base coat.

   5. Using a softening paintbrush, blend brushstrokes if necessary.

2. Frottage the Ginger Jar

1. Gently place a sheet of tissue paper over wet mixing glaze/paint mixture.

2. Using a cloth and your fingers, press the tissue paper to wrinkle. Remove immediately and discard.

3. Repeat as necessary until entire outer surface of ginger jar has been patterned. Let dry.

3. Seal the Ginger Jar

1. Using a 1" China-bristle paintbrush, apply a generous coat of water-based varnish to ginger jar to seal. Let dry. To achieve a high-gloss finish, apply two additional coats and let dry after each application.

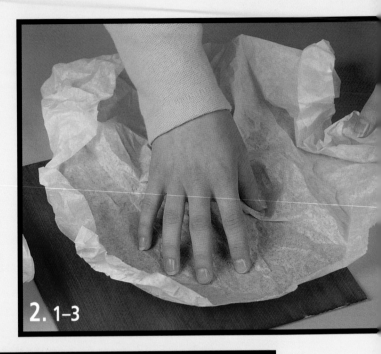

2. 1–3

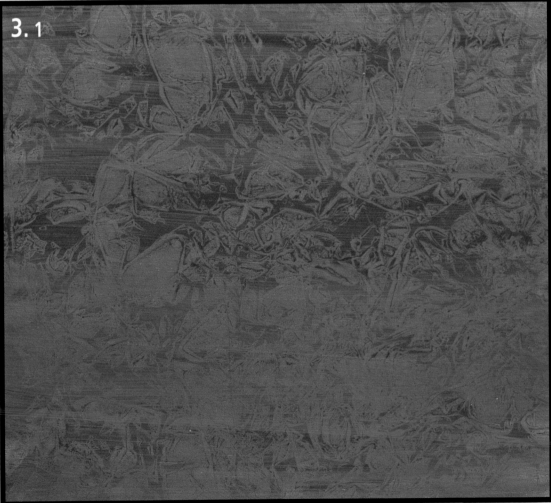

3. 1

80

How do I achieve the look of tortoiseshell using paint?

Tortoiseshell, first used as a veneer or thin overlay to decorate small areas, gave way to the creative paint finishes of the expert craftsperson. Early versions of this tradition were rendered in a natural, imitative style. Today, this technique enjoys a whimsical approach and can be found on a variety of surfaces.

**What You Need
To Get Started:**

Acrylic craft paints:
    metallic gold; grape;
    red-orange; rose;
    soft yellow
Craft sticks
Disposable cups
Mixing glaze, clear
Paintbrushes:
    $1/2$" flat stiff-bristle;
    1" flat China-bristle;
    1" flat soft-bristle;
    #0 liner
Plastic scouring pad
Primer
Rubbing alcohol
Water-based varnish,
    satin finish
Wooden tray,
    unfinished

Tortoiseshell Tray

Here's How:

1. Paint the Tray

1. Prepare tray, following How do I prepare surfaces for faux finishing? Wood instructions on page 17.

2. Using a craft stick and a disposable cup, mix soft yellow paint with a few drops of water-based varnish.

   Note: The consistency of this paint/varnish mixture should be that of medium cream.

3. Using a 1" soft-bristle paintbrush, apply a coat of paint/varnish mixture to tray. Let dry.

4. Using a plastic scouring pad, lightly buff tray.

5. Apply a second coat of paint/varnish mixture. Let dry.

2. Add the Tortoiseshell Finish to the Tray

1. Using a craft stick and a disposable cup, mix equal parts of mixing glaze and metallic gold paint. Mix well.

2. Add a few drops of water to mixing glaze/paint mixture.

   Note: The consistency of this mixing glaze/paint mixture should be that of ink.

3. Add a few drops of rose paint. Mix well.

4. Add a few drops of red-orange paint. Mix well.

5. Using a 1" soft-bristle paintbrush, apply a generous coat of mixing glaze/paint mixture to tray, working small areas at a time.

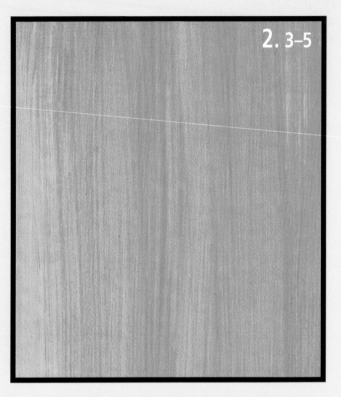

2. 3–5

6. Using a ½" stiff-bristle paintbrush, spatter droplets of rubbing alcohol onto tray, over wet mixing glaze/paint mixture.

7. Using a #0 liner paintbrush, add droplets of rubbing alcohol onto tray, over wet mixing glaze/paint mixture.

   Note: The rubbing alcohol will cause the mixing glaze/paint mixture to pull into circles and rings exposing the base color. If the ringed areas pull back in on themselves, it may be necessary to wait a few minutes, then reapply droplets of rubbing alcohol.

8. Continue until surface of tray is covered. Let dry.

9. Using a craft stick and a disposable cup, mix equal parts of mixing glaze and grape paint. Mix well.

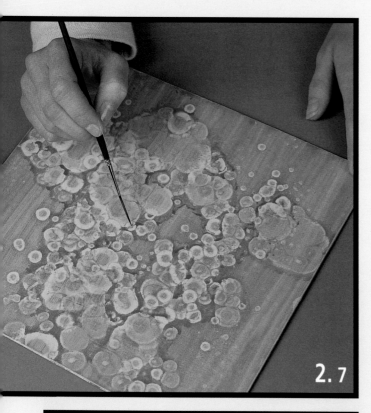

2.7

10. Add a few drops of water to mixing glaze/paint mixture.

    Note: The consistency of this mixing glaze/paint mixture should be that of ink.

11. Using a 1" soft-bristle paintbrush, apply a generous coat of mixing glaze/paint mixture to tray, working small areas at a time.

12. Using a ½" stiff-bristle paintbrush, spatter droplets of rubbing alcohol onto tray, over wet mixing glaze/paint mixture.

13. Using a #0 liner paintbrush, add droplets of rubbing alcohol onto tray, over wet mixing glaze/paint mixture. Let dry.

3. Seal the Tray

1. Using a 1" China-bristle paintbrush, apply a generous coat of water-based varnish to tray to seal. Let dry for 24 hours. Apply a second coat and let dry.

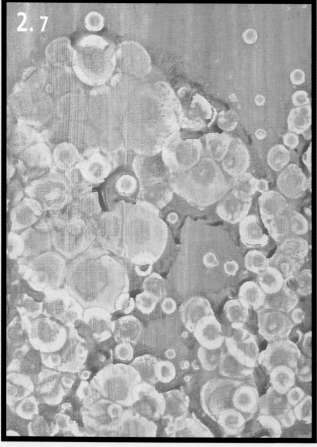

2.7

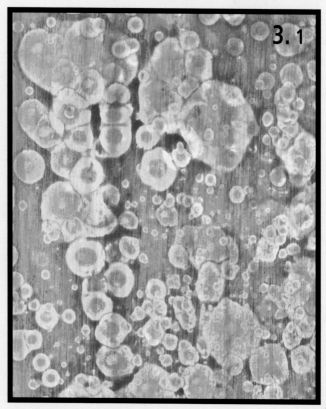

3.1

How do I achieve the look of marble using paint?

Marbling is the most sophisticated of the faux-painting techniques. Its timeless, decorative quality lends formality to traditional surroundings or a sleek, stylish look to modern decor. With thought and imagination, a truly effective marbled look can be achieved.

What You Need To Get Started:

Acrylic craft paints:
  dark blue;
  burgundy;
  metallic gold;
  off-white; white
Craft sticks
Disposable plates
Mixing glaze, clear
Natural sea sponge
Newspaper
Paintbrushes:
  ½" flat soft-bristle;
  ½" flat China-bristle;
  #0 liner;
  softening
Primer
Water-based varnish,
  high-gloss finish
Wooden chairs

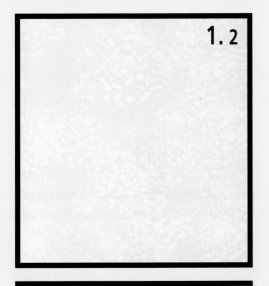

1. 2

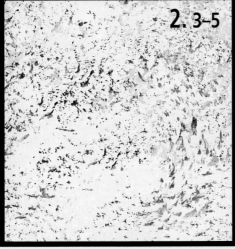

2. 3–5

Marbled Chairs

Here's How:

1. Paint the Chairs

    1. Prepare chairs, following How do I prepare surfaces for faux finishing? Wood instructions on page 17.

    2. Using a ½" soft-bristle paintbrush, apply a base coat of off-white paint to chairs where marbling finish is to be applied. Let dry.

2. Sponge-paint the Chairs

    1. Using a craft stick and a disposable plate, mix two parts mixing glaze with one part white paint. Mix well.

    2. Thoroughly wet and wring out a natural sea sponge.

    3. Refer back to the following steps on page 43 for Technique 9: Sponge-paint the Stand, Steps 3–5.

4. Using a craft stick and a disposable plate, mix two parts mixing glaze with one part dark blue paint.

5. Sponge-paint chairs, over mixing glaze/ white paint sponged areas. Leave patches of white paint exposed.

6. Using a craft stick and a disposable plate, mix two parts mixing glaze with one part metallic gold paint.

7. Sponge-paint chairs, over mixing glaze/ dark blue paint sponged areas. Leave patches of each color exposed. Let dry.

3. Marble the Chairs

1. Using a #0 liner paintbrush, drag a burgundy paint line across surface to create "veins."

2. Using a softening paintbrush, gently brush across wet veins.

4. Seal the Chairs

1. Using a ½" China-bristle paintbrush, apply a generous coat of water-based varnish to chairs to seal. Let dry for 24 hours. Apply a second coat and let dry.

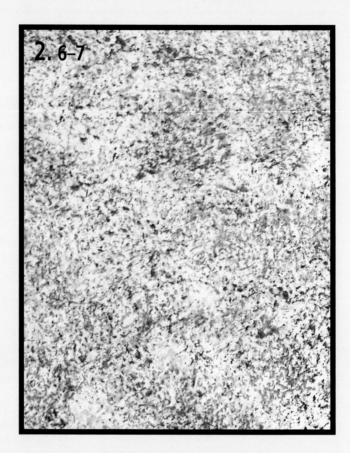

2. 6–7

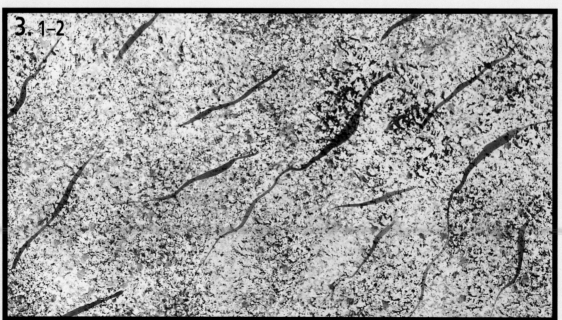

3. 1–2

How do I create wood grain using a wood-graining rocker?

The art of imitating wood grain with paint is a fairly recent development in the history of faux painting. Early craftspersons used paintbrushes to apply the pattern, now a "magic" tool called a wood-graining rocker can be used to replicate the texture of wood.

Wood-grained Box

Here's How:

1. Paint the Box

1. Prepare box, following How do I prepare surfaces for faux finishing? Wood instructions on page 17.

2. Using a craft stick and a disposable cup, mix equal parts of light tan paint and water-based varnish. Mix well.

3. Using a 2" China-bristle paintbrush, apply a generous coat of paint/varnish mixture to box. Let dry for 24 hours. Apply a second coat and let dry.

4. Using a craft stick and a disposable cup, mix five parts mixing glaze with one part light brown paint. Add a few drops of water. Mix well.

   Note: Mixing glaze/paint mixture should hold its body and not be too runny.

5. Using a 1" soft-bristle paintbrush, apply diluted mixing glaze/paint mixture to box, over base coat.

Note: When applying a wood grain finish to a box, work only one side at a time.

6. Using the bristle tips of a 1" soft-bristle paintbrush, gently brush wet mixing glaze/paint mixture to smooth and remove lines.

2. Apply the Wood Grain to the Box

1. Using a wood-graining rocker, slowly and gently pull toward you in a rocking motion from front of curve to back. Begin at the top of the area to be wood-grained and proceed in the direction you choose the wood grain to go.

   Note: Always work with the direction of the grain.

2. Using a damp cloth, wipe wood-graining rocker at the end of each "stroke."

2. 1

3. Repeat until all desired box surfaces have been wood-grained. Let dry for 24 hours.

   Note: If a softer look in the wood grain is desired, lightly drag a 1" China-bristle paintbrush through the wet mixing glaze/paint pattern.

3. Seal the Box

1. Using a 1" China-bristle paintbrush, apply a generous coat of water-based varnish to box to seal. Let dry for 24 hours. Apply a second coat and let dry.

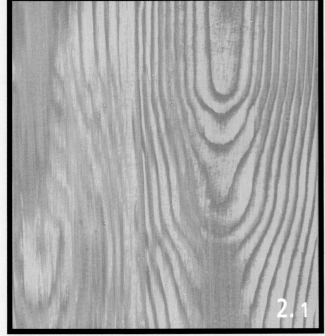

2. 1

Design Tip: Check the surface of your project before beginning. If the surface is uneven, the wood-graining rocker will leave an uneven pattern.

3. 1

24
technique

What You Need To Get Started:

Acrylic craft paints:
  black; metallic gold;
  red; dark tan;
  light tan; medium tan
Craft sticks
Disposable cups
Disposable plate
Mixing glaze, clear
Newspaper
Paintbrushes:
  ¼" flat stiff-bristle;
  1" flat China-bristle;
  #0 liner;
  #2 round soft-bristle;
  #8 scumbling;
  softening
Plastic scouring pad
Primer
Sponge, synthetic
Tack cloth
Water-based varnish,
  elite diamond finish
Wooden lamp,
  unfinished

How do I achieve the look of bamboo using paint?

Bamboo, a woody grass, has been used as a popular, oriental theme for centuries. There are hundreds of different species and many colors, giving the artist and craftsperson many choices when creating exotic decor. The painting style chosen for this lamp originated in 20th-century Paris.

90

Faux Bamboo Lamp

Here's How:

1. Stipple the Lamp

1. Prepare lamp, following How do I prepare surfaces for faux finishing? Wood instructions on page 17.

2. Using craft sticks and disposable cups, mix three parts mixing glaze with one part paint for each of the following colors: light tan, medium tan, and dark tan.

3. Refer back to the following step on page 46 for Technique 10: Stipple the Candleholder, Step 4 (includes photograph).

   Note: Blend and feather edges. Let dry until slightly tacky.

4. Using a 1" China-bristle paintbrush, apply a generous coat of water-based varnish to lamp to seal. Let dry for 24 hours.

2. Spatter the Lamp

1. Slightly dilute black paint with water.

2. Load a ¼" stiff-bristle paintbrush with diluted black paint.

3. Refer back to the following steps on page 22 for Technique 1: Spatter the Bowl, Steps 1 and 4 (includes photograph).

   Note: Spatter should be heavier at "joints."

3. Sponge-paint the Lamp

1. Using a craft stick and a disposable plate, mix two parts mixing glaze with one part black paint. Mix well.

2. Thoroughly wet and wring out a synthetic sponge.

3. Refer back to the following steps on page 43 for Technique 9: Sponge-paint the Stand, Steps 3–5.

   Note: Sponge-paint at "joint" areas. Let dry.

4. Add the Detail Painting to the Lamp

1. Using a craft stick and a disposable cup, mix equal parts of black paint and water. Mix well.

2. Using a #0 liner paintbrush, paint "Y-shaped" spines in an off-set, irregular pattern around bamboo joint. Spines coming from the bottom ring should point down and spines coming from the top ring should point up. Taper the tail to a fine point. Let dry.

3.3

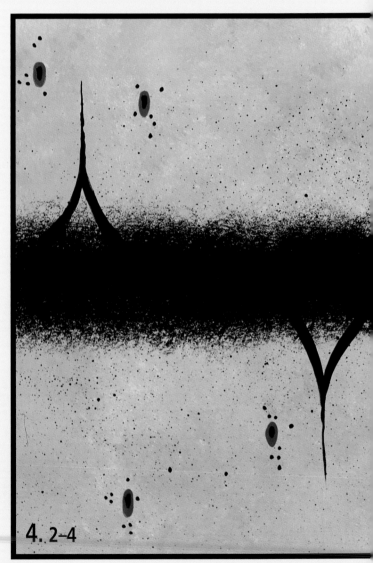

4.2-4

4. Using a 1" China-bristle paintbrush, apply a generous coat of water-based varnish to lamp to seal. Let dry for 24 hours.

3. Using a #2 soft-bristle paintbrush and red paint, paint small ovals (eyes) at irregular intervals, near, but not touching the spines. Let dry.

4. Using a #2 soft-bristle paintbrush and black paint, place a small dot slightly off-center within each red "eye." Make various-sized dots, clustered in threes or more close to the eyes. Let dry.

5. Using a 1" China-bristle paintbrush, apply a generous coat of water-based varnish to lamp to seal. Let dry for 24 hours.

Design Tip: Applying a coat of varnish after each application of paint gives a lovely, deep lacquered finish to the project.

---

5. Re-spatter the Lamp

1. Slightly dilute metallic gold paint with water.

2. Load a ¼" stiff-bristle paintbrush with diluted metallic gold paint.

3. Spatter the lamp.

6. Seal the Lamp

1. Using a 1" China-bristle paintbrush, apply a generous coat of water-based varnish to lamp to seal. Let dry.

2. Using a plastic scouring pad, lightly buff lamp.

3. Using a tack cloth, wipe lamp to remove excess dust.

4. Apply a second coat of varnish. Let dry.

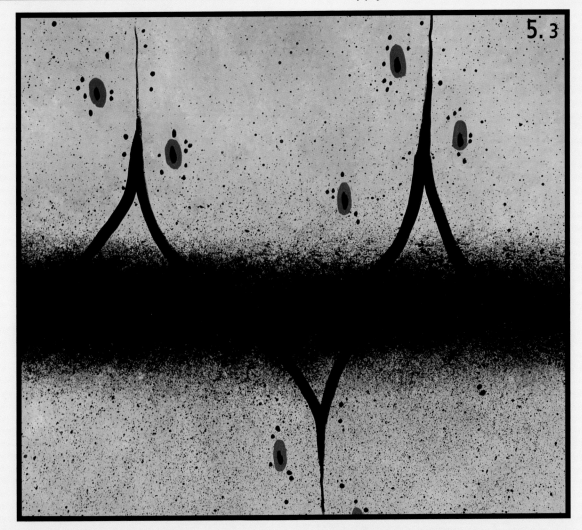

5.3

Created by Jimmie Emmett

Created by Jimmie Emmett

Created by Jo Packham

PRIVATE

94

Courtesy of Sargent Architectural Photography

Created by Russell J. Stettner

Section 4:
gallery

Created by Jer Giles

Created by Tish Inman

Created by Tish Inman

Jer Giles grew up in Huntsville, Alabama, and received a Bachelor of Fine Arts Degree in Theatrical Design and Production from the University of Texas. In 1979, Jer became an independent business owner and in 1982 he crossed the footlights, painting magic in homes, offices, and restaurants around the country. In 1986, he developed a niche in the decorative arts and established Jer Giles Artworks, Inc. In 1997, he founded the Academy of On-line Muralists, an international group of artists that communicate over the Internet.

Jer Giles is a decorative artist with a dramatic attitude. Trained in the European style, with a distinctive American flair, it is his theatrical training that propels his work into the extraordinary. Whether it is a faux finish on a wall, a mural in the dining room, or a custom finish throughout the house, the overall feel is one of natural beauty created by a skilled craftsman, not by some formula-driven application.

His work has been published in numerous local, state, and national magazines. In addition, Jer has appeared on television shows demonstrating his techniques.

As a professional artist, Jer has been creating magic in homes throughout the Dallas/Fort Worth metroplex. When his clients build or remodel their homes, Jer is there to bring his talent to the job. Working closely with the builder and designer, together they create the necessary ambience.

Created by Jer Giles. An al fresco touch to this dining room mural opens up the small dining area. The opposite wall is mirrored so the reflection is seen in the entry and living room.

Created by Jer Giles. The jungle mural is the focal point of this dining room. Faux stone columns in the entry, two-color glaze on the walls, and a pastel sky painted in the vaulted ceiling enhance the dining experience.

Tish's clients are not a swarm of unknowns viewing a static display of her creations. They are newly made friends who live in and around her work in every room of their homes: from basement to bedroom, rec room to restroom. But always, they are treated to a glimpse of the islands she loves. They are surrounded by the warm sun, the shifting sea, the ever-changing sky, and the bold colors of the plants and flowers. They are treated to a taste of a vibrant blend of the forever stimulating, yet tender, tones and feelings exclusive to her beloved land—Trinidad.

Tish Inman was born Martitia L. Inman in Korea with itchy feet, doodling fingers, and an unbridled imagination. So, it was no surprise to her parents when at the tender age of seven, Tish announced that she wanted to become an artist.

Tish obtained a Bachelor of Fine Arts Degree from Norfolk State University in Virginia in 1980. She viewed her degree as an end which signaled a beginning—now she had permission to demonstrate what she knew.

Her disobedience to the norm manifests itself, not only in the content of her artwork, but in the context as well. She has not formally exhibited for a while. Instead, her artwork can be enjoyed in numerous households and businesses along the Eastern Seaboard of the United States of America.

Time spent in Trinidad, beginning in 1981, brought out her best. It was there that she found inspiration and solace, knowledge and wisdom.

Created by Tish Inman. This Oriental carved table is a great representation of faux marble.

Created by Tish Inman. This vintage bathtub is striking with the faux malachite finish.

Created by Tish Inman. This bathroom is breathtaking with its use of tile and the faux marble columns.

Created by Tish Inman. This foyer is elegant with the use of faux marble columns and the rich burgundy glaze that has been applied to the walls.

Created by Jimmie Emmett. The floor of this foyer was created with faux marble, trompe l'oeil, and faux mosaic on concrete.

Jimmie Emmett creates and implements interior and landscape designs, and is noted for his trompe l'oeil and faux finishes. He has received favorable notice in *Southern Accents* and *Southern Living* magazines, and was named by the *Washingtonian Magazine* as one of the best faux artists in the region. He was also recently featured in an HGTV Bed and Bath Design segment.

His commissioned paintings, interior designs, trompe l'oeil, and gardens are enjoyed by private owners from South Beach, Florida, to Quechee, Vermont.

He is currently creating a line of furniture featuring faux inlay and finishes.

New clients are his greatest challenge and he hopes one day to find the time to work in his own garden.

Created by Jimmie Emmett. The floor of this tasting room, located above the wine cellar, was created with faux cobble on concrete.

Created by Jimmie Emmett. Architectural trompe l'oeil with hand-painted panels, gold leaf, and faux marble grace this sitting room.

Natalie L. Herman lives and works as a decorative artist in Toronto, Ontario. She began her own decorative painting business in 1990 by combining her background in Fine Arts and Design Arts.

Natalie's paint finishes can be seen in numerous homes and businesses. With her repertoire of paint finishes, Natalie has decorated the surfaces of lobbies, boardrooms, several model homes and suites, salons, health clubs, retail stores, showrooms, and the Air Canada executive departure lounge.

Her talents have been volunteered to Toronto's Ronald McDonald House and the Bob Rumball Center Manor House for the blind.

Natalie has made several guest appearances on the Life Network's "Just Ask" and "Free for the Asking" television programs. She has also been featured on the television program "Lynette Jennings Home" and her work has appeared in several *Style at Home* magazines.

In addition to creating painted finishes for both commercial and residential clients, Natalie conducts weekend workshops in faux finishing for do-it-yourselfers.

Created by Natalie Herman. Smoky blue venetian plaster and iridescent top coats were applied to this floating curved wall. Custom-stenciled "squares" wrap around the top of each stone-finished column.

104

Created by Natalie Herman. Layers of copper and gold are color-washed over the walls of this cozy sunroom.

Created by Natalie Herman. A wainscoting of dry-brushed "diamonds" was created for this dining and living area.

Created by Natalie Herman. A softly painted sky was created within this ceiling alcove overlooking the dining room table.

Created by Natalie Herman. This model suite was treated to a "fresco" finish using glazes of bronze and golden yellow.

107

Russell J. Stettner is the artist and president of Russell Joseph Studio, Inc. Russell was born in New York and has been a resident of Florida since 1980.

Russell has been creating and designing finishes for over 13 years. He has studied in New York under Ina Brousseau Marx of The Finishing School along with Gary Finkle and Clyde Wachsberger of Tromploy, Inc.

His professional skills include: glazing, stucco lustro Veneziano (a technique brought from Italy consisting of layers of polished colored plaster), marbling, gilding, stenciling, neoclassical designs, wood finishes (including wood graining, wood staining, and hand-rubbed finishes), antique finishes, and trompe l'oeil.

Russell's work has been published in *Architectural Digest, Florida Design Magazine, Showhouse Magazine*, and *Gold Coast Magazine*. He is currently a member of the local chapter of the Industry Foundation of the American Society of Interior Designers (ASID).

His work may be appreciated in such places as the Kravis Center for the Performing Arts in Palm Beach, Bank Julius Baer of Palm Beach, Knox Theological Center of Fort Lauderdale, and the Rose Institute of Fort Lauderdale, as well as many estates and exclusive homes along Florida's coastline.

Russell has participated in and donated his services to the 1994 Jr. League of Boca Raton Showhouse, the 1995 Jr. League of Fort Lauderdale Showhouse, the 1997 Jr. League of Fort Lauderdale Showhouse, and the 1997 Red Cross of Palm Beach Showhouse.

Created by Russell J. Stettner. The grandeur of this foyer is enhanced by the glazed walls, faux marble trim, gilded soffit, and faux marble columns.

Created by Russell J. Stettner. This dining room with teal blue walls, done in a soft mottled glaze, is enhanced by the contrasting furnishings.

Created by Russell J. Stettner. This fireplace was white plaster before being transformed into a masterpiece.

Metric Conversions

INCHES TO MILLIMETRES AND CENTIMETRES

MM-Millimetres   CM-Centimetres

INCHES	MM	CM	INCHES	CM	INCHES	CM
1/8	3	0.9	9	22.9	30	76.2
1/4	6	0.6	10	25.4	31	78.7
3/8	10	1.0	11	27.9	32	81.3
1/2	13	1.3	12	30.5	33	83.8
5/8	16	1.6	13	33.0	34	86.4
3/4	19	1.9	14	35.6	35	88.9
7/8	22	2.2	15	38.1	36	91.4
1	25	2.5	16	40.6	37	94.0
1 1/4	32	3.2	17	43.2	38	96.5
1 1/2	38	3.8	18	45.7	39	99.1
1 3/4	44	4.4	19	48.3	40	101.6
2	51	5.1	20	50.8	41	104.1
2 1/2	64	6.4	21	53.3	42	106.7
3	76	7.6	22	55.9	43	109.2
3 1/2	89	8.9	23	58.4	44	111.8
4	102	10.2	24	61.0	45	114.3
4 1/2	114	11.4	25	63.5	46	116.8
5	127	12.7	26	66.0	47	119.4
6	152	15.2	27	68.6	48	121.9
7	178	17.8	28	71.1	49	124.5
8	203	20.3	29	73.7	50	127.0

YARDS TO METRES

YARDS	METRES	YARDS	METRES	YARDS	METRES	YARDS	METRES	YARDS	METRES
1/8	0.11	2 1/8	1.94	4 1/8	3.77	6 1/8	5.60	8 1/8	7.43
1/4	0.23	2 1/4	2.06	4 1/4	3.89	6 1/4	5.72	8 1/4	7.54
3/8	0.34	2 3/8	2.17	4 3/8	4.00	6 3/8	5.83	8 3/8	7.66
1/2	0.46	2 1/2	2.29	4 1/2	4.11	6 1/2	5.94	8 1/2	7.77
5/8	0.57	2 5/8	2.40	4 5/8	4.23	6 5/8	6.06	8 5/8	7.89
3/4	0.69	2 3/4	2.51	4 3/4	4.34	6 3/4	6.17	8 3/4	8.00
7/8	0.80	2 7/8	2.63	4 7/8	4.46	6 7/8	6.29	8 7/8	8.12
1	0.91	3	2.74	5	4.57	7	6.40	9	8.23
1 1/8	1.03	3 1/8	2.86	5 1/8	4.69	7 1/8	6.52	9 1/8	8.34
1 1/4	1.14	3 1/4	2.97	5 1/4	4.80	7 1/4	6.63	9 1/4	8.46
1 3/8	1.26	3 3/8	3.09	5 3/8	4.91	7 3/8	6.74	9 3/8	8.57
1 1/2	1.37	3 1/2	3.20	5 1/2	5.03	7 1/2	6.86	9 1/2	8.69
1 5/8	1.49	3 5/8	3.31	5 5/8	5.14	7 5/8	6.97	9 5/8	8.80
1 3/4	1.60	3 3/4	3.43	5 3/4	5.26	7 3/4	7.09	9 3/4	8.92
1 7/8	1.71	3 7/8	3.54	5 7/8	5.37	7 7/8	7.20	9 7/8	9.03
2	1.83	4	3.66	6	5.49	8	7.32	10	9.14

Index